WIRED FOR WONDER

WIRED FOR WONDER

THE THEATRICAL SCIENCE OF MAGICAL PERFORMANCE

MASTERING ACTING, STORYTELLING, AND STAGECRAFT

by Tobias Beckwith

Including interviews with
Phil Ackerly and Douglas Conn

Triple Muse
Publications

Copyright © 2025 by Toby L. Beckwith. All rights reserved.

No part of this book may be used or reproduced in any manner whatsoever without written permission except in the case of brief quotations embodied in critical articles and reviews.

For information, visit www.triplemusepublications.com
E-mail: tobias@wizardventure.com

Book design and layout by Tobias Beckwith

www.tobiasbeckwith.com

Published by Triple Muse Publications

Library of Congress Cataloging-in-Publication Data has been applied for.

ISBN: 979-8-9926512-1-8

Table of Contents

Introduction 1
1: Varieties of Magic Theater 7
2: What Makes a Good Story 57
3: The Art of Performing Magic 67
4: Show Tech 103
5: The Team 111
6: Putting it all Together 123
7: Theater Adjacent: Shows Online . 129
Conclusion 141
End Pages 144
Index 146

Introduction

Do you remember the first time you stood before an audience? Not just your parents or siblings, but strangers—faces you couldn't quite read? I do. I was doing a book report on the first book I ever bought: *The First Book of Magic*. My teacher suggested that instead of writing a summary, I might perform some of the tricks. I jumped at the opportunity. I remember feeling nervous, convinced the tricks wouldn't actually fool anyone.

But they did. The response was electric: applause, laughter, a feeling of adulation I'd never experienced. Afterward, I was transformed, elevated to a status that seemed impossibly grand for a first-grader. I was hooked. The connection formed with a live audience resembles nothing else in human experience. That is the magic of theater.

This book is about that intersection—the specific theatrical craft practiced by performing magicians. It draws from years spent working in the theater—first at the college level, then on and off Broadway, and later alongside some of the world's finest magicians.

Theater is defined as what happens when live performers stand before a live audience of any size. Magic is, therefore, theater. More importantly, theater belongs to the storytelling arts, and all great storytelling is inherently magical.

I actually "gave up" magic for years because, as it was often practiced, I didn't find it very magical. I was far more deeply moved by novels, films, and theater. They transported me into enchanted worlds and provided truly magical experiences. Many magicians I encountered seemed only interested in tricking me; this was mildly amusing, but not worthy of a life's dedication. I didn't realize then that I simply hadn't met the right magicians. The "right" magicians understood that their goal wasn't just to fool an audience or deliver an evening of amusement. Their singular goal was to create a magical experience. Magic is fundamentally about transformation, and transformation comes about when we experience moving stories—especially those that force us to question the limitations of our perceived reality.

If your response to that is that you're not a storyteller, I beg to differ. Here's why: Whenever a performer confronts a live audience, what the audience takes away is a narrative. Event A happens, then Event B, then Event C. That chain of events is a story. Therefore, they will get a story even if you aren't consciously creating one. Because both performer and audience are live and in person, the experience and the resulting memories are profoundly different than if the same story were written or seen on a screen. Although fiction, film, and theater all tell stories, live theater is special because it is inherently interactive. Communication flows both ways, which makes the audience a more integral part of the story than in any other medium.

There is one crucial factor particular to magic we must be aware of: Performing magic is a special case in that it often eliminates the "fourth wall." In conventional theater, this invisible wall separates the action on stage from the safely insulated audience, who remain observers, not participants. Magic shatters that wall. We actively "break the fourth wall," meaning our audience members are no longer passive spectators; they become characters and active participants in the narratives we are telling. Unlike actors on stage who have rehearsed their lines, the audience members at a magic show are making it up as they go. This is a vastly different situation. What's more, the narrative your audience takes away isn't about fictional characters—it's a story that happened to them!

So, how do you ensure the theatrical experience you create is a powerful one for both you and your audience? We must consider the full range of elements that define a theatrical production. There is always a script, because things happen in a particular order. When performing, you are always acting, portraying a character, using your voice and body, and connecting with that audience. There is almost

Introduction

always light, which can enhance performance, and sound—sometimes just your voice and props, but often a musical underscore. Visual elements (costume, props, and setting) are nearly always involved. Performances occur in diverse venues, ranging from cocktail parties and family living rooms to giant theaters and arenas—and the chosen venue heavily influences the experience possible. Every single element affects the final result.

You can be a magician without memorizing a script or overtly telling a story, but your audience will still experience a narrative. Consider: "She was dressed in black. When she came in, she had a deck of cards in her hand, and she asked us…" At that point, you are already in a story. There is no escaping it. Your job is simply to ensure the story they take away is a good story!

The story is the essential basis for the magical experience. We will begin by discussing what constitutes a strong theatrical story, focusing on narratives most effective for live audiences. We will determine the kinds of stories we want to tell with our magic. The book then covers critical performance skills: acting, voice, movement, and improvisation. Finally, we move on to basic stagecraft, including set, props, costumes, sound, and lighting, and how to collaborate with others to ensure all aspects of your performance are the best they can be.

I am fond of the idea that all art is fundamentally about making choices. The visual artist chooses subject, color, style and composition; the musician selects rhythm, melody, and harmony; the choreographer works with music and the human form. In theater, we combine all these arts, giving us many more options. This is both a blessing and a curse. Why?

It's a blessing because every choice grants you control that can make the experience more magical. The curse is that your audience experiences those choices even if you haven't consciously made them. For example, if you habitually wear torn jeans and perform an elegant, Lance Burton-style dove magic act without changing, the audience sees

Wired for Wonder

a "kid in torn jeans." This creates a specific effect, whether you intended it or not. Are you using a prop decorated with Chinese characters while telling a story about raising chickens on a Kansas farm? The Chinese box sends a conflicting message, creating cognitive dissonance that detracts from the desired effect. EVERYTHING COMMUNICATES.

It would be a mistake to think there is only one kind of magic theater. In fact, there are many, each with a distinct purpose and different conditions of performance. Before diving deeply into the art of theatrical storytelling, we will examine the different types of performance environments magicians may encounter.

Jean Eugène Robert-Houdin famously wrote, "A conjuror is not a juggler. He is an actor, playing the part of a magician." Magicians often repeat this quote, but I wonder if we truly grasp his original intent. I would rephrase the quote for the contemporary performer: A magician is a very special kind of storytelling performer, playing a character with magical powers. Because the magician stands before a live, human audience, magic is undeniably a form of theater. It is a unique form, however, because magicians utilize tricks and illusions to present a version of the world that seems impossible. Magicians differ from most other performers because we must consistently 'break the fourth wall' and draw our audiences in as other characters in the play we present.

This is more essential to our art than you might imagine. I've seen numerous Broadway shows and movies featuring magic effects, but almost none succeed in making the audience believe the magic, except for dedicated magic shows. As soon as the magic retreats behind the fourth wall, the audience sees it as a special effect—part of an imaginary world they are not directly experiencing. This can still be effective theater, but it is no longer magic, at least not the kind that drives a magician.

In the coming pages, I will describe the many different kinds of magic shows that work successfully. They all share two fundamental

Introduction

things: The magician treats the audience as essential participants, as characters in the story being acted out. They also ask the audience to believe—they do not ask them merely to *suspend* their disbelief, as is common in most dramatic forms.

Wired for Wonder

Chapter 1
Varieties of Magic Theater

Magicians, as we noted in our introduction, are different from other performers in that we must 'break the 4th wall' and acknowledge our audience as another character in the play we present. Another way of saying that is that we insist on stepping out of the traditional "story world," and into the audience's own world.

Let's have a look at some of the different forms this unique kind of theater can take.

Dante, Blackstone - Magic in a Big Theater

I couldn't have been more than five or six years old when my parents announced they were taking my brother and me to a magic show. It would be at the big pavilion of the Chautauqua Institute, about a 45-minute drive from where we lived. I knew about magic from the stories my parents would read us at bedtime, but had no idea how it might be part of a show. If I had those magical powers, I didn't think I'd use them just to put on a show. Still, if I could encounter someone with real magical powers, I was interested.

This was in the late 1950s, and some of the great magicians from "the golden age" of magic were still touring. Our magician was one of those, though I've never been able to find out which one I saw. From what I remember of his appearance, I'm guessing it was either Blackstone or Dante.

We dressed up in our Sunday best, piled into the car, and drove to Chautauqua. The Chautauqua Institute was located on Lake Chautauqua, a small lake just south of Lake Erie. It was well-known as

Wired for Wonder

a cultural center, presenting speakers, musicians, and performers like the magician we saw that day.

This turned out to be what I think of as the classic magic show. The stage set depicted a fancy Victorian drawing room with ornate furniture, heavy draperies, and gilt-framed art. I'm sure there was a large oriental carpet. The magician was dressed elegantly in top hat and tails.

This was not a huge production magic show by today's standards. There may have been one or two assistants, costumed as servants in a Victorian household would have been, but no dancers or large cabinet illusions. I remember the magician making silks vanish and having them reappear out of various vases and other objects around the stage. The show was basically a demonstration of various parlor tricks, without additional story. I suppose it may have been amazing to some, but as a five-year-old looking to experience real magic, I found it disappointing. It was certainly polished and elegant... but boring.

Not too many years after this, I discovered an aging copy of Professor Hoffman's **Later Magic** in the library and read it cover to cover. It was there that I learned this sort of elegant drawing room magic had been a huge draw back in the late 1800s and early 20th century. But even by the late 1950s, when I saw it, the show seemed tired and slow-moving, at least to my five-year-old sensibilities. I think my parents were disappointed and a bit baffled by my indifference.

Having been raised on bedtime stories of real wizards and sorcerers, someone doing a card trick or making silks vanish and reappear seemed anticlimactic in the extreme. Reflecting on the show now, I suspect part of the problem was that it was designed for a smaller venue, and I was seated too far from the stage.

Just a few years later, Doug Henning and David Copperfield moved beyond this format and created genuinely entertaining theater with their magic in large venues. They weren't the first to do large illusions in theatrical touring shows, but they were the first ones I got to see, and

Chapter 1: Varieties of Magic Theater

both were very much rooted in contemporary culture, whereas that first show was more of a throwback to the late 1800s.

Today, I think David Copperfield's show is the standard bearer for big-theater magic. There are huge illusions that fill not just the stage but other parts of the theater as well. Even with all the grand spectacle, it is David's dreams and personality that inspire the show and make it succeed. This was the same for the Siegfried and Roy show, which was perhaps the biggest spectacle ever created as a magic show. Sure, there were amazing illusions and giant spectacle, but they're very much in the service of the magician's persona, and that's key to the success of this kind of show. Without it, the show falls flat, no matter the amount of spectacle.

Uncle Bob - The Original Stroller

If you ask a hundred young magicians about when they first encountered magic, about half will probably tell you, "My uncle pulled a coin out of my ear." There is apparently something about that particular moment - and trick - which seems to catch our attention and interest like no other. Perhaps it has something to do with it being a surprise encounter with magic. Because we weren't expecting it, the magic is somehow more powerful. It is something that happens to us, not something we observe, which in some ways makes it quintessential "magic theater."

I have to wonder if it might also be because it is also a demonstration of a kind of power at a time in a young person's life when they might be feeling powerless, and beginning to look for ways to build their own sense of power. I know that as a young boy, this was definitely one of the things which attracted me to performing magic, and from long observation of many magicians, I have to say that a lot of us never do move beyond that stage of "I know how it's done, and you don't."

This brings us to the theater of one-on-one interactive magic. As a young man, I often got together with a friend or two and shared card tricks. The theater of this kind of magic seems to be more about fooling your friends and learning how to fool your friends than it does about interesting or powerful magical stories and experiences.

Still - all the elements of theater apply. There is a venue - often Mom's living room, or the kid's own room. There are props - cards, coins or other simple magic props. There is "one who knows" and "one who is fooled." These are characters with motivating needs - usually to "be the cool one" who knows how the magic works, but also to "fool my friends," or to "figure out how it's done." Costumes, story, lighting and sound are all present, but seldom actually a consideration for either the performers or audiences.

The one-on-one nature of this early experience of magic is, however, one that never leaves us. Many magicians make it a point to have what Jeff McBride refers to as their "every day carry," a bit of magic they can perform anywhere and at any time. They might pull it out over a drink at a bar, or while waiting for a server to bring food in a restaurant. At its best, this magic provides amusement, an experience that will kick off a discussion, or just acts as a kind of gift the magician gives. In the overall scheme of things, this may be the most performed kind of magic in the world. If you're reading this book, it is the magic you are most likely to perform!

Beyond that, this kind of one-to-one or one-to-a-few style of magic is the variety of magic most professionals most often get hired to perform! Corporate parties, private events like weddings, and more, will often hire you to perform strolling magic at their events. In Las Vegas alone, there are probably at least 100 such parties almost every night.

What, then, are the theatrical considerations of doing one-on-one magic? One is certainly the story your audience will take away from the performance. I have a vivid memory of Jeff McBride, early one morning as we were about to leave for the airport for an out of town performing gig, performing magic for our taxi driver as he was about to help us load Jeff's props into the back of his car.

Chapter 1: Varieties of Magic Theater

This guy was a recent immigrant from Haiti, and had never seen this kind of magic before. But apparently he was a strong believer in real magic, including voodoo. He was terrified when the magic happened - I think it was Cards from Mouth - and jumped into his taxi and drove away making signs against the evil eye. We had to flag down another taxi. So make sure you have some idea of your audience's preconceptions and beliefs about magic before you inflict it upon them! I expect the story that taxi driver took away was something like, "I met a devil!"

Cards from the Mouth, like Coin from the Ear, is one of those sudden magical experiences that comes without warning. Sometimes it's better to make sure you know who you're performing for before offering up something quite so shocking. For the right audience and at the right moment, there are few more effective bits of magic out there.

This brings us to a consideration which is especially relevant to this "one on one" or "one to a few" that you encounter when doing strolling magic: You really need to know your audience! The slightly off-color bit of "surprise" magic that might be perfect for a group of guys at the bar will not do well at all for the society reception at the local country club. Remember, in our special form of theater, your audience is also a character in your performance, and you'll want to make sure you don't cause them to react in ways that will damage the overall effect of the performance! You also want to be careful that you don't ask them to play a role that makes them uncomfortable.

Once you know your audience, as a strolling magician you'll need to put together a half dozen or so bits of small magic that you can easily carry on your person. You'll want pieces that don't require complicated set-ups, because when you're strolling you won't be able to go backstage and reset them in between the groups you perform for. You don't need a lot of pieces, because you'll be performing short sets - from 5-15 minutes - again and again for different groups. Still, you need a strong opener and strong closer and one or two pieces that play well in between. Ideally, your bits need to work with or without a lot of audience involvement. Every group will have different ideas about the

Wired for Wonder

degree to which they want to participate, and you need to have material set for every eventuality.

Tableside Magic

Imagine reserving a table at Chicago's most elegant restaurant. Upon being seated, the Maître D' informs you, "Tonight is a special night here at Biggs. Our favorite magician is visiting. You may have heard of him—Eugene Burger. If you would like—and only if you like—we can ask Mr. Burger to come to your table after we've served your dessert, and I can promise you'll have a wonderful time with him!"

That was how diners at top establishments in Chicago were introduced to magical theatrics for several decades at the end of the 20th century and beginning of the 21st. Eugene, with his big voice and amazing beard, would come to the dinner table, be seated in the place of honor, and proceed to charm and amaze everyone. This was magic "up close and personal." The magician knew your name and made you a part of the magical stories. As a spectator you would participate, selecting cards, holding props, and Eugene would include everyone in the experience. Always charming, he was also mysterious, funny—and amazing! A set of close-up magic with Eugene at the table was a wonderful and exclusive experience for all.

I was fortunate to be one of Eugene's friends and to teach with him at the McBride Magic and Mystery School. One of Eugene's secrets, often imparted to our students, was that magic should always be something more than "the adventures of the props in the magician's hands." Props needed to take on personas, to function as metaphors in a larger story. Still, "first you must deceive." The magician's job was to provide a magical experience—something more than just a puzzle to be figured out.

As for a venue, this was a dinner table in a popular restaurant. His purpose was to make an already wonderful evening even more of an unforgettable experience for all. The restaurant loved him, because once their high-society clientele experienced Eugene's shows, they

Chapter 1: Varieties of Magic Theater

would always want to bring their friends back to share the special experience. Eugene himself had another purpose—it's okay to have more than one. He not only wanted to make the clients feel they had an amazing and delightful night out at the restaurant, but also wanted to get at least one additional gig as a result of his performances on any given evening.

Many restaurant magicians "work for tips." Eugene did not. "If they tip me $20, then in their minds, I'm a $20 magician. I couldn't have that. So when offered a tip, I'd just say, 'Thank you so much. They actually compensate me very well here. But I know John, your wonderful server this evening, would really appreciate that added to his tip!'" Eugene didn't need the $20, because he was angling for the $2,500 gig at the country club event that the client might be hosting later in the month!

As a performer in a restaurant, you'll need a set of props you can easily carry with you. You'll have to find ways of handling them and transitioning between pieces smoothly that are quite different from stage performers. You'll need to make sure you're performing at just the right place at a table, next to the guests you want to interact with, and a place with sufficient table space and light to make your presentation easily experienced by all. You'll be working in what is sometimes a noisy restaurant situation, and so you must consider using simple language that everyone at the table will be able to understand, even in that environment.

Not every restaurant magician will have the luxury that Eugene Burger did of being specially introduced by the host. Many times you'll have to introduce yourself and find a creative, fun way to do so. You'll have to recognize that your services at a table will not always be welcome and have a graceful way to leave when that's the case. In other words, you'll need to consider the overall situation in which you are performing. How does your magic enhance the overall experience of that restaurant, both for those who work there and the clientele? Are you making things easier or harder for the servers and the host? Are you enhancing the experience for the diners, or bothering them? Are

Wired for Wonder

you spending too much time with one table, leaving others who might be interested in seeing your magic frustrated because you've ignored them?

Before moving on, I should note that different restaurants will have different needs you can satisfy. Some, like the ones Eugene Burger performed at, want you as that special something extra that will keep their clientele coming back again and again. Others want you there to entertain the kids while the family is waiting for dessert. I know magicians who were hired by super popular restaurants where people might wait upwards of 30 minutes to be seated, just to keep those in line entertained so they wouldn't get impatient and go somewhere else. Be sure you have a discussion with whoever hires you about just what sort of problem you're solving for them and what they would see as a big success.

Kids & Family Shows

Let's hire a magician for little Timmy's birthday! Or for our anniversary party! This is generally a show stringing together lots of magic with audience participation, all performed in someone's living room or back yard. Honestly, I suspect most people encounter their first magician at one of these events. Some magicians love doing this kind of shows, but if you're a full time professional, you have to do a lot of them to make a decent living. The upside of that? You get to do lots of shows!

Here are the particular challenges that family show entertainers will face:

First, you'll never be in the same venue twice in a row. Every show will require you to set up stage, audience area, etc. You will probably have to bring all the tech equipment you use, and set it up and tear it down yourself, often with the audience already in the room with you. You'll be performing for many people who have never seen a live show of any kind before, and have no idea about what the proper etiquette is for that. They'll talk over you, run across your "stage" during the show, and find a hundred other ways to distract. But it's all part of the

Chapter 1: Varieties of Magic Theater

experience, and if you can learn to enjoy the wide-ranging interactivity, family entertaining is hard to beat.

I'm fortunate to be friends with one of the top family entertainers in the world, specifically in the San Francisco Bay area, and he has agreed to share some of his knowledge here.

Phil Ackerly, a five-time "Best Entertainer" award winner, brings his captivating blend of magic, comedy, and fun to audiences across Northern Nevada and California. Phil expertly unites guests in joyous, shared experiences, conjuring up laughter and amazement whether for birthday parties or public "Home Edition" shows. He's also the author of "Magic Tricks for Kids".

More than just tricks, Phil is a master showman dedicated to creating unique and memorable experiences for everyone. He engages all ages, from children to grandparents, making each guest feel special with personal touches and humor for every generation. Phil believes the real magic is the shared joy and lasting memories created, aiming for guests to leave feeling transformed and connected.

Interview with Phil Ackerly

TOBIAS: The new book is *Wired for Wonder: The Theatrical Science of Magical Performance.* The thing I haven't done much is what you've done most: family performances in living rooms, backyards, restaurants. What are the considerations in that situation?

PHIL: Theater can be something as simple as a three-by-three-foot space where you're standing with someone doing a trick. It could be anything you want.

Home parties are different. Every home, backyard, or park presents a completely different venue. Unlike a permanent theater where I know the exact lighting and entrance, every home venue is completely different.

What I've learned is to own my space. Someone once told me, "Own the stage. It's your stage. Own it." A magician once said that if a client wants me to set up somewhere that won't work,

Wired for Wonder

I tell them, "If you let me set this up the way I need to, I'll give you the best show ever, but I need your help." They usually respond with, "Whatever you need."

When I go into someone's home, the first thing I do is look at the space. I always set up away from the traffic flow. If I'm in a room with multiple entrances, I want to be on the opposite side of the main entrance. I avoid setting up next to the door, the food, or any high-traffic area.

I keep my props hidden away. If I have a table with a prop, I'll put it behind a curtain, then bring it out when it's time. This is like the "portal" you told me about. It elicits curiosity—"What's that?"—as opposed to having it already there and losing that initial wonder.

TOBIAS: Magic props draw attention just by themselves because they're so weird.

PHIL: Let's face it: we play with toys. I call it eye candy. They're colorful and fascinating. So again, it all comes down to owning your stage, creating your stage.

I remember when Jeff McBride was setting up at Apple. We asked him, "Can we have all the kids sit up front?" He replied, "No, no, no. Let the kids sit with their parents. I don't need a mosh pit of kids high on sugar in the front."

Having all the kids out front with parents in the back makes it feel like a kids' show. Jeff wasn't doing a kids' show. Having kids with their parents is great because they're less likely to shout things, and they're spread out. It all comes down to managing your space.

TOBIAS: Do you have a sound system built into your table?

PHIL: I do. It's all battery-powered and self-contained—old computer speakers I took apart and put into the box. The setup needs to be simple. I want to roll in with the music and amplifier already set, put out one table, and I'm ready to go

Sometimes with sightlines, you just have to deal with what you've got. I was doing a show and was about to do my final trick, the bunny rabbit production. I heard someone say,

Chapter 1: Varieties of Magic Theater

"Well, we've got to go now." In my head, I thought, "She's going to walk right past me to the front door." So I decided to engage her. "Oh, you can't leave yet. What is your name?" I started asking her questions, and she stayed through the whole thing. When the bunny came out, she exclaimed, "Oh, I'm so glad I stayed!"

TOBIAS: You're touching on something I feel strongly about: the family show is the quintessential version of magic differing from other theater because the audience *is* the other character. You're always relating directly to them; there's no fourth wall.

PHIL: Sometimes you have to consider whether to ignore something because it might destroy the moment you're trying to create. But I think it's great when you interact and react to what's happening in the room; it makes you human. But you need to stay in control.

TOBIAS: Your example showed you can be in control without being macho or overbearing. You can be gentle and interact on a heart level.

PHIL: You still need to maintain control. I've had a kid say "Boo, you suck!" right in the middle of a show. I stopped and said, "Excuse me, what did you say? No, we don't do that in my show." I take ownership. Afterwards, his mom brought him up, and he apologized.

Another time, I was about to produce the bunny. I looked through the window and saw someone walking up. As I was about to produce it, I opened the door, put the box right into her arms, snapped my fingers, and she opened the drawer. The bunny jumped out. Everyone was freaking out, and I just made that a moment in the show. The key is to not flinch, go with it, and make it part of the show.

What I don't like are magicians who are so conversational that the audience interrupts them. I want to be in theatrical control. It's a show. So if a kid says something, I'll react, but I don't want to lose focus.

I took improv classes. One time, I told a kid to "take the magic wand." The kid said, "That's not a magic wand. That's just a stick." I used my improv skills: "Oh, you're right. It is a stick. Okay, take the stick." The kid couldn't react because I didn't argue. You disarm the kid.

When the kids are up front and the adults are in the back, it's important that I address both. What I find really important is eye contact. I'll look down and talk to the kids, but I also look over their heads to the back of the room. My goal is to keep everyone engaged.

TOBIAS: I think it's important that if you're sitting in the last row and I look at you, you feel engaged and seen.

PHIL: If it's a kid's birthday party, the kids will obviously be engaged, but I always want to involve the adults. Eye contact is super important.

TOBIAS: You have flashy tricks but also tell stories. How do you determine the mix?

PHIL: Your show has to have nice flow, nice texture. I have a flashy opener, then a personality piece, followed by a flashy piece with colorful scarves. Then I bring a kid up. After that, a fun torn-and-restored toilet paper routine. I might do a storytelling piece in the middle to bring the energy down. For adult shows, I'll stop and talk about myself: "I was born and raised in the Bay Area, used to work in high-tech, then got laid off and became a full-time magician." That's storytelling, and it gives them background on me. I think it's important to open up to the audience.

TOBIAS: Your bunny piece is a storytelling piece with big spectacle and an emotional hook. I think it's one of the reasons you work pretty much whenever you want.

PHIL: When I get to my bunny routine, I walk over, slide the chair to center stage, and sit down. The audience wonders, "What's he doing?" I pause. Then I say to the kid, with all sincerity, "Tobias, thank you for having me at your birthday party. I really appreciate it. When I was your age, we didn't have magic shows. My parents took me to San Francisco to see Blackstone the magician." What's great is that when I'm telling the story, everyone goes quiet. You once told me

Chapter 1: Varieties of Magic Theater

storytelling is hypnotic. I've had a room full of kids going bonkers, and now they're all silent.

TOBIAS: It's amazing you can do that in somebody's living room with five-year-olds.

PHIL: I've learned not to prejudge my audience. I'll get to a party and kids will be going bonkers. I'll think, "This is going to be a disaster!" But as soon as the show starts, they're angels. If I tell myself it's going to be a disaster, it will be. Try not to prejudge.

TOBIAS: How does your audience know when the show has begun?

PHIL: First, I have background music playing. The music stops. Then I stand in front and ask, "Are you guys ready for the show?" I add, "It's not just a show for the young, but for the young at heart!" Then I hit my remote: "It's showtime!"

Before starting, I tell them: "Stay seated on your bottoms. Crisscross applesauce. I need a volunteer, but I don't pick hands. I pick smiles!" Then I have a voice-over that introduces me. I also use a bell gimmick that becomes part of the opening routine.

My opening bit engages the kids, but also the adults in the back. My goal within five minutes is to let the adults know, "This is for us, too." The best comment I get afterwards is, "Wow, even I had fun!"

My job in five minutes is to connect with everybody. On a big stage, if a group tunes out, it doesn't affect everyone else. But at a home party, everyone can hear and see everyone.

TOBIAS: When you start your show makes a big difference.

PHIL: Sometimes you have to start during dessert. You just have to be flexible. That's one difference from a theater show: I have more distractions.

Sometimes when people walk in late, I'll say, "Oh, you're just in time." If someone else comes late, I'll say it again—it becomes a running gag. If someone comes really late, I'll act

Wired for Wonder

surprised: "You just missed the Bengal tiger!" And the kids will shout, "Oh, it was awesome!" Everyone's involved in the gag.

You have to make distractions work for you. I was doing a show in a park when all the kids looked to my left. I turned around: there was a chicken walking behind me. I had to acknowledge it. "Hey, I'm working solo! Get out of here! This is the first time I've ever been upstaged by a chicken!"

TOBIAS: How many family shows have you done in one day?

PHIL: Six shows twice. The sixth show was at 9:00 at night. The important thing is that the sixth show gets the same energy as my first. The adrenaline just starts flowing.

TOBIAS: One magical thing for theater performers is that you get energy back from the audience. Family audiences are almost the best for that.

PHIL: You might feel exhausted before you go on, but the juices start to flow, and it's back and forth.

TOBIAS: Mac King's show is pretty much the same every time, except for the eight or nine people he brings onstage. He'll say, "I couldn't do it without that interaction. That's where the magic really happens."

PHIL: If I had to do the same show for 15 years, it would get tough. I've been doing birthday parties for 35 years. What keeps it fresh is that I can change tricks, always putting something new in. It's those moments of interaction that are golden. My goal is always to maximize the reaction. You're always looking for ways to improve. That's what keeps you going.

TOBIAS: You can experiment because you're building on a foundation you've created. You don't truly get to be in control until you've rehearsed it so much that you don't have to think about it.

PHIL: You know what will get applause, which gives you confidence and allows you to play. I think it all comes down to owning your stage, owning your show, owning those

Chapter 1: Varieties of Magic Theater

moments. People come to see you; they expect you to be in charge. The audience wants you to succeed. You've already won half the battle.

TOBIAS: Let's talk about show length and purpose.

PHIL: For family bookings, how long is a good show? The answer depends on the performer. While 55 minutes is somewhat long, if you have texture and variety—storytelling and silent interaction—then 55 minutes flies by.

I have different packages. For a four-year-old's birthday, I do 30 minutes. For a home party with younger kids, 45 minutes is good. At preschools, 25 minutes is the limit. Around that mark, I get the kids to stand up and move. Then they sit down, and we continue.

TOBIAS: Why work this market?

PHIL: It keeps you honest. You can't fake connections; you'll know right away if you've lost them. I love the variety. What's the purpose? I put that back on the client: what are you trying to accomplish? But for me, the purpose is to create a show that not every magician can do. It comes down to creating memories. I want to make it unique so they don't leave saying, "Oh, we saw that trick before."

Casino Showrooms & Theaters

Much of my friend Jeff McBride's career was built on performing his unique stage show in casino showrooms, for audiences made up of those who visit places like Las Vegas and Atlantic City to gamble and indulge in other "adult" activities. Our audiences in those venues were considerably different from the ones in cabarets in New York or theaters we would play when on tour. Jeff liked to describe them as either "thinking" or "drinking" audiences, and the shows for those two had to be quite different. Casino audiences were definitely of the "drinking" variety.

Our shows were particularly popular in casinos because they were not your typical illusion show. While other illusionists wheeled in boxes on wheels, stuffed them with dancers in scanty, sparkly outfits, and did

Wired for Wonder

"impossible" things to them, Jeff performed in whiteface makeup not unlike that of the rock group Kiss, and combined his amazing sleight of hand skills with pantomime, Kabuki stylings and magical stories from many cultures. Every performance piece had its story, and the emotions ranged from mysterious to touching to hysterically funny, and at times, even terrifying.

The real reasons casinos loved the show, though, was that it was easy for them to publicize using unusual, dramatic visuals, it always came in at the requisite 70 minutes, and sent audiences back out onto the casino floor buzzing with excitement. Excited customers tend to lose more at the tables and slot machines. So for us, doing a great show was certainly satisfying — but the real success of the show for the casinos was its ability to draw those audiences and excite them.

Whatever kind of magic you want to do, it will pay you to know what it's really for from the perspective of those hiring you and the audiences you work for. If you want professional success, this is an important distinction: those who hire you might have quite different criteria for judging success than the audience you perform for. You must satisfy both.

If you're going to be performing in casinos, you need to be aware that you'll be performing on well-equipped stages with stagehands and crews provided by the casino. You might bring one or two of your own illusion show stagehands with you, but by and large you'll need to learn to work with that local crew. Most casino showrooms have extensive set lighting already hanging in the room, which can be supplemented. If you have your own lighting designer you can bring with you, that will go a long way to making things go more smoothly and creating a better show than if you have no idea about the intricacies and nuances of effective stage lighting. Similarly, if you've worked out all of the details of how props and illusions get on and off stage before you arrive at the casino, this will save hours of technical rehearsal for your show. In casinos and stock theaters, it's more important than any other kind of magical performance that you understand all of the different elements

Chapter 1: Varieties of Magic Theater

available to you to enhance (or detract from) your performances, and are prepared to deliver on every one of those with the same artistry and professionalism that you would expect from a Broadway show or touring Pop star.

A bit of advice here - don't just understand how the technology - lights, sound, projections, etc. - work. It's not enough to know how to run the lightboard or sound board. You also need to understand what you want the lighting (for example) to look like, and why it needs to be that way.

I once worked in China with a brilliant lighting artist used to working for rock bands. He could deliver some truly amazing lighting effects. The problem was trying to perform a magic show in the middle what was essentially disco club lighting. That made it very difficult for the audience to pay attention to the performance we were putting on. I had to demand, again and again, that he save his fancy dancing light cues for certain spots in between our performance pieces. He finally understood, but it was a struggle!

Street Performance / Busking

I have the greatest respect for those who are able to build a career performing on the street. It is the one part of the performance world where you don't need to be hired, and don't need advance marketing, don't need a support team. You do need a great, not too long show that can draw and hold an audience on a busy street corner or in a park. You need to be able to attract the attention of people who probably had no intention of stopping to see a show, and probably have somewhere else they need to be. You need to be able to make them want to stop, make them want to stay, and make them want to leave you a tip when it's all over. There is no safety net. As a performer, you live and die in the moment. You need to provide an experience that is better and more exciting than whatever all those people passing by had in mind for themselves before they encountered you.

If you have what it takes to do that on the street, you can probably

Wired for Wonder

hold and please an audience in almost any other situation. Street performing will teach you more about your real-world business as a performer in just a few weeks than a four year college degree will!

That said, what sets this form apart from magical performers in theaters, at cocktail parties or in other places? One is that you are not just the performer in this situation. You have to deal with creating the space for the performance, marketing and selling your performance even as it is beginning, managing the audience as they drift in and out, and motivate them to pay you when they really have no obligation to do so. You basically create the business, deliver the product, and collect your reward in the space of an hour or so — and then go on to do it all again an hour later!

I'm not a street performer, but I have many friends who are, or have been, so I got in touch with one of the best, Douglas Conn.

Interview with Douglas Conn

TOBIAS: Tell me how you got started in magic and then street performing.

DOUGLAS: I was inspired to do magic by a grandfather who did some simple sleight of hand. I transitioned to magic kits and Bill Tarr's magic books, which were wonderful. I stuck with magic through childhood, utilizing libraries. When I was about 16, I found a magic shop and learned about performers like Harry Anderson and Penn & Teller. I also heard Robin Williams and Amazing Jonathan were street performing. I heard about these guys who would take their acts out onto the street and perform them.

I actually ran away from home at age 16 to be a street performer at Panama City Beach, but I failed miserably. That was my earliest attempt at being a busker.

In 1987, I met Jim Cellini at a bar called "Buskers," where he held a convention featuring amazing magicians. More importantly, it had Jim and a host of his close friends. Cellini was certainly one of the most prominent street performers

Chapter 1: Varieties of Magic Theater

ever, probably the best street magician from this country, and perhaps the best street magician ever to live.

TOBIAS: That sounds like an amazing event.

DOUGLAS: At this convention, there were probably 20 top-tier street magicians and buskers. That was all the inspiration I needed to know I wanted to try street performing again. This origin story also had a lot to do with me crossing paths with Tom Frank. I was 18 years old and attending the Taste of Cincinnati, a small food festival in Cincinnati, Ohio.

I saw Tom Frank street performing out there and he invited me to share a pitch with him. I did the next day, and I never went back to work. That summer, I would be on a bus to Chicago, which led me to New Orleans, where I was a street performer for 30 years.

TOBIAS: That is a great story. One of the things this book is about is what makes a good story. One of the elements is that you clearly enter what I call "story space". There is a point when you are in the theater, you get to your seat, the lights go down, the curtains open, and now you are in a different world. On the street, you do not have those clues to help you. What do you do to get your audience to know they are experiencing something out of the ordinary?

DOUGLAS: It is a little bit different than normal theater because no one buys a ticket. The buy-in begins the moment you are able to capture one passerby's attention. Step one is always to take someone from their everyday life and bring them into yours. This often requires bravado and confidence. A flashy and quick magic effect always helps, but it is not necessarily definite. You can also set the mood with music, which creates a theatrical ambiance.

TOBIAS: Music makes a bigger difference than most people realize.

DOUGLAS: In general, a few quick words and a general sense of positive energy draws them in. I always say confidence is the most important thing. You start a show by being confident about the situation, and your audience feels secure that they are with a professional. We have our well-scripted opening lines and hooks. We know how to command our audience, giving them directions. A theater might be built on the street, for example, by drawing a chalk line or setting out a rope. We invite them, "Hey, put your feet up to the rope or get right here on the trap door". We make some fun banter and again command our audience what to do.

TOBIAS: I see.

DOUGLAS: Here is a hot tip where everyone fails at street performing. Right out of the gate, we tell them what to do. We do not ask them, "Would you like to see some magic?" or "Would you like to come a little closer? You will see better". I don't think so. We are not giving them a chance to make a choice. We are telling them it is going to benefit them, so that makes sense.

TOBIAS: I think that is true for all performers. I know that was always one of Jeff McBride's secrets: always commanding his audiences. They don't have a lot of choice in this.

DOUGLAS: It is especially true when you are working any environment where you are strolling, interrupting, or invading a personal space at a restaurant. You had better be commanding that situation, and questions are generally bad.

TOBIAS: Absolutely. I know when I teach public speaking, I tell people they need to get this through their head: You are the one in the front of the room, which means you are the boss. You have to live up to being the boss.

DOUGLAS: If you don't, you are going to have chaos. Even more so on the streets, you will have anarchy. Complete control is a necessity.

TOBIAS: Exactly. How much do you mix up pieces where you are just performing with ones that involve the audience? Juggling is a spectacle, but it might not involve any audience members. However, working with rope or cards usually involves audience members directly. They are holding things, standing on stage with you. How do you determine that mix?

DOUGLAS: The older I get, the more audience involvement happens for me. I encourage all performers working in magic

Chapter 1: Varieties of Magic Theater

to involve the audience. When buskers ask me, "How can I make my show better?", I say, "Instead of projecting your magic to an audience member in front of you, invite the audience member to be with you on the stage".

It is like Nate Leipzig's approach, where the audience watches the interaction between you and the spectator on stage versus you doing the magic at them. They experience a different kind of theater.

TOBIAS: I always feel that is something magic has that is really special in the world of theater. With most theater, I can sit in the dark with my arms crossed and watch the action happen. But in magic, I am involved as an audience member, if only because I am trying to figure out "How did he do that?" or "Why did she do that?". It is a different kind of audience involvement than in regular theater. Another way of saying that is that magic is unique in the theater because the audience is inside the fourth wall—they are both observers and characters with us. They do not have the option of sitting back in the dark and just watching.

DOUGLAS: Yes. The more of that, the better. I do not add a new piece to my act now unless that is happening. If I am considering a new moment for any piece—street theater, stand-up, close-up—the audience must be involved. When I was a younger magician, I thought the role of the magician was to demonstrate wonderful powers and how great the magic is. To some effect, that does work; you can do that and get by. However, if you want to do magic at its highest art form, your audience needs to be as involved with the magic as possible. People love to watch people, and when the magic is happening with a spectator, it is always elevated.

TOBIAS: One of my themes here is purpose: "What is it for?" It is easy to answer that if I am a trade show magician. I know I am there to gather audiences, qualify them, and send them into the booth. If you are a casino showroom performer—and most of them do not know this—you are there to generate publicity for the casino, to get audiences into the casino. You get them into your showroom for an hour or 70 minutes, not longer, and send them back out on the gambling floor more excited than when they walked in,

27

Wired for Wonder

because excited people gamble more. We know these are the purposes for those performances. What is the purpose for a street performer?

DOUGLAS: Before I talk about doing it for money, let me say that street performing can be one of the purest ways to express your art, get repetitions in, develop an act or any performance piece you are working on, and generally just to share wonder and joy in the world. You can just go out there and do magic in the wild. There is no better way to do it when that happens. So often, as magicians, we are invited to perform in environments where we do need to interrupt people, or we are not the focus of attention, and magic is just a sub-part of the event. When you are on the street and you stop people in the wild, and they make the choice to come to you in that moment, it is the purest form of expression for magic I have ever discovered.

So, the purpose of street performing is to give genuine magical connections in the purest way possible. No tickets were purchased. I did not have to interrupt you at dinner. I am not bothering you as you are at the bar at the Pepsi Corporation event. We are in a park, and you said you would like magic in your life, and you liked me enough to do these three things. This is what Cellini taught at his first lecture when I saw him. Street magic is three things: you make them stop, you make them stay, and then you make them pay. Assuming you do this for a living, that is the role of the busker as a professional: make them stop, make them stay, and make them pay. There are 8,000 things that fill in the gap of doing those things correctly, but that is the short form summary of what street magic is about.

TOBIAS: I understand. Ultimately, that is kind of what every kind of storytelling is about. I am reading another book right now on how your brain is wired for story, *Wired for Story* by Lisa Kron, and one of the themes is that we all love stories. We love reading or being told stories, but most of us do not know how to create stories. She says you are just not wired that way. Ultimately, the key is that at every moment, the readers have to want to know what is going to happen next.

Chapter 1: Varieties of Magic Theater

"He did this. Now what is going to happen? And **then** what is going to happen?".

DOUGLAS: That is so important. Once we get them to stop, we create anticipation of the big final moment. We get them to stop, we get them to stay, and we are saying, "See that straitjacket? I am going to get in that straitjacket and be bound up in that, and you will be amazed by what happens then. You are going to want to see that. But first, pick a card. And by the way, I am not paid by the city, the state, or any other evil organization to be here today". We work in our money pitch and start priming the pump so that they will be happy to reward us at the end of the show.

TOBIAS: Great.

DOUGLAS: You are so right about storytelling—that makes all of that work. I was watching Winston, a local street performer in Las Vegas, out on Fremont. He said, "I am out here, one day hoping to be in there" and he turns and points at the casino. "I have been doing this since I was 16". He tells his story to the audience about what he is hoping to accomplish as a young performer. Then the audience is so behind supporting this kid. They want to help this kid get there. If you are firing on all cylinders and giving a good performance, and back it with stories and authenticity, you are going to succeed.

TOBIAS: I like that you are clarifying that you are basically weaving the threads—the anticipation—all the way through from the beginning.

DOUGLAS: If you are just out there hopping from one tip to the next, you will have limited success and probably get by. But if your show has drama and builds, if there is conflict in there, that is different. Maybe you borrow some money and it burns, or even just having an audience member on stage with you creates some form of conflict for the audience to enjoy perceptually.

All the theater elements are important. Probably even more so on the street because there is no room to be subpar if you want to do it as a professional.

TOBIAS: Yes.

DOUGLAS: You have to be great. You cannot be a poor performer and have a good life. You cannot miss out on any of your three points, or any of the other 8,000. You have to be able to gather a crowd. If you cannot hold a crowd, if you cannot make them pay, you are going to be hungry. Most buskers I know are always working to improve. You are never finished. I feel that way for most art, and magic in general is like that. We can always improve the moments. Every second can be analyzed.

It is nice to be working in an environment where you are not only getting the repetitions but you have the eyeballs of other performers and constructive feedback on a daily basis, not just from your audience. Hopefully you are recording the shows and taking notes, getting the benefit of doing five or 10 shows a day, which is the highest benefit of street performing if you are developing as a performer.

TOBIAS: This is good stuff, but let's move on. What are the best pitches, or locations, you have ever encountered—best places to perform as a street person?

DOUGLAS: It is hard to say the best place to go, but in general, it is best to be the big fish in a small pond. I was told, "Go to New Orleans. That is the place to be. You will see da da da and there, right?". But where it was great for me was when I first started. I did not know what I was doing out of the gate. I had trained a little with Tom Frank. I had gone to Chicago. I killed it. I was the only magician. In fact, I was one of a few street performers in a very robust area. So, I was the big fish in the small pond. I was the only one working.

Then I went for the winter to New Orleans, where I proceeded to make about a third of the money I had in Chicago. This was because I was in a queue with four other magicians and the tourists all had their heads on a swivel. Everyone has their hand out. It is not like Chicago, where it is a little more refined and city-like. It is kind of gritty, with homeless people, scammers, shoe shiners, and 20,000 buskers instead of three. So, in general, try to be unique in your spots,

Chapter 1: Varieties of Magic Theater

but ultimately you have to be able to do it all because it is rare that you can work just one spot and be a successful professional.

You are going to have to travel, and it is always going to change. If you find one good spot, because it is good, it will be ruined over the course of a year or two or three, because the other buskers will find out. On that note, we won't say too much about what the good spots are right now. I will get in trouble from the other buskers.

TOBIAS: Certainly. Let's go the other direction then. What is the worst pitch you ever worked?

DOUGLAS: Probably New Orleans. It is the best of worlds and the worst of worlds. I have had some of the best work in my life there. But if you really want the worst pitch ever, go do a couple hours on Bourbon Street between 6:00 and 8:00 PM and see how your old magic show goes there.

TOBIAS: More drunks per square foot than any place on the planet.

DOUGLAS: In my early years in New Orleans, it was a necessity for me to make that money because you can earn an income working those hours. But you better have your big boy pants on if you are going to go show card tricks on Bourbon Street.

TOBIAS: I bet you get accosted by all those bad elements you mentioned before.

DOUGLAS: And they will all be intoxicated. The tourists have no filter. But sometimes they tip you heavily.

There are problems where it is overcrowded with performers. For example, if you go to Key West, there are two hours to perform, and there are 20 performers, and you are literally shoulder to shoulder. So, you might be out there doing cups and balls and you are right next to a guy on a 20-foot tightrope. It is a different problem in that you have to be the best performer because your visual elements and tricks are not going to make a difference. Your storytelling had better be top tier.

Wired for Wonder

TOBIAS: Do you use sound equipment on the street?

DOUGLAS: I use amplification when needed. I do not like to use it and prefer an environment where no one is amplified, but for most of my life, I have had to, because New Orleans is loud. We have brass bands and break dancers with huge amps and musicians everywhere, and crowd noise on the streets. Once one person turns on an amp, the next one turns it up a little higher, and when the break dancers show up, you can hear them three blocks down the street.

So, yes, I do. But I recommend not using it. If a student is really interested in busking, they should start without it to develop the vocal muscles necessary. It is really necessary. You will lose your voice if you are not used to working without one and then you travel—because we have to travel and then if this city does not allow it, you might not be able to work because your vocal cords are not able to handle the stress.

TOBIAS: Let's talk about how you structure your show. What kind of material works? What do you open, close, and middle with? What are your thoughts about, for example, if someone is just starting out and wants to build a show as a street performer?

DOUGLAS: We can reflect back to a good flashy opener. I work in two styles. I will do a bigger show, a half circle for about 50 to 100 people, or I will do a close-up walk-around, a close-up stroll by, which is about a 5 to 7 minute experience. That is actually my preferred way of working these days, but that is another snowball to open because now I am integrating social media with street performing—which is another whole ball of wax.

The approach I would advocate to anyone interested in the subject, and how I would approach it these days, would be to start with a flashy opener. This is after stopping one or two people. What I use for that is often just a thumb tip and a silk. I look for a family and say, "Hey, watch this!". I give them a five-second quickie. Boom, boom, boom. If I can get an affirmative, positive response, I go on: "Hey, you like that? Stand here". Now it is showtime. "Okay. So, hey folks, we are going to start a show. You will want to see this". At this point,

Chapter 1: Varieties of Magic Theater

I get a flashy prop out. For me, that is normally the linking rings. In my opinion, the rings have all the perfect elements for the street. People know it is a magic trick. They know you are not scamming them. They see these big silver things.

To echo Cellini, it has the elements of sound, movement, and color. When he lectured on the subject, these were the elements he suggested were extremely important: sound, movement, and color. The rings have all of this. Cellini had all of it in his costuming and in his props. But in an effect alone, the linking rings with their clash, clash, clash—"Here, hold this". The people are examining the rings, and now we have interest, and it is building. So now we have maybe 10 or 15 people. At this point, I would choose a middle piece, and it depends on the size of the audience. Rope magic is a great choice. These days I am generally doing a ring, rope, and a sensational piece.

I open with rings. My middle pieces start with rope, and I might integrate some B pieces, some coin magic in there. I am a pretty flexible magician. As a wiser magician, I can extend the show to 25 minutes or keep it down to 12 or 15 minutes, depending on the situation.

TOBIAS: Okay, so you would open with rings and then move to ropes. Let's talk a little bit about the length of your show.

DOUGLAS: I might lengthen or shorten the show as needed depending on audience interest, or if I want to build a bigger crowd. I would use other effects accordingly, like coin magic and/or card tricks. My traditional close for a bigger show is the cups and balls.

TOBIAS: Excellent.

DOUGLAS: These days I very much prefer to do seven to 10 minutes intimately. That show is mostly coin magic, sponge bunnies, and a multiple selection card routine. For me, the income is about the same, and I can do four or five shows in the same time it takes to do one or two. I am generally able to work more flexible spots doing that style of magic. Good spots are often overcrowded by big acts, jugglers, straitjackets, break dancers, and now you have to wait an hour or two or

Wired for Wonder

three in between your performances. So, you might make one hundred or two hundred per show, but if you want to do three shows, you are out there eight hours.

So I can go to work at like 9 or 10 in the morning and be done by 1:00 PM, doing close-up magic with the other system. I actually prefer to do close-up as opposed to a bigger theater show. When we talk about integrating the audience, they are all 100% there. My audience is just one foot from me at all times.

TOBIAS: That is a useful observation—that the smaller, closer audience is far more involved than, say, the one in Radio City Music Hall. It is a completely different experience.

DOUGLAS: When I learn your name and say it, if I ask you to pick a card—and when I do a multiple selection trick where I have eight people pick a card—eight people feel intimately involved in the experience. When I suggest a $20 tip at the end of the show, they are more likely to give that amount. The large audience performers will suggest a $20 tip, and they will get it from the guy they borrowed the bill from for the bill and lemon trick, because he is intimately involved. But will five other people give you a $20? Maybe. I know from experience the tips get higher in a more intimate setting.

TOBIAS: I am hearing that there are actually different styles of street magic?

DOUGLAS: Yes, there are several theater styles on the street. That is one of them. Some guys do walk around. They walk up to people, and that is an intimate way to work, although it can feel a bit repetitive. That would drive me crazy to do the same trick walking around all day.

Then other guys do even bigger shows. Some magicians work out of their pockets and do 45 minutes in Jackson Square. Guys like Alexander Osborne and Nico Leo are out there doing borrowed bill routines, some rope magic, and some great coin and card stuff. They command the largest audiences. They are circling them in the middle of the most challenging venue on the planet and paying them. They probably make upwards of $300 to $500 per show and are

Chapter 1: Varieties of Magic Theater

earning a pretty good living doing exactly what they want, when they want.

TOBIAS: That is great. It is interesting to me because in the book I am defining street performing, close-up magic, and these large overarching categories. But every kind of magic has a big range within it.

DOUGLAS: I have seen guys do dove acts out there. I have seen guys do escapes or Metamorphosis illusions. I have even seen mentalism on the street. I would not want to do it, but Mick Stone was crushing with it, mainly doing Q&A. Again, we are involving those spectators. He will go, "Here, write down a question. Write down a question". Now everyone has skin in the game, as they say. That is so important.

TOBIAS: I was teaching a workshop a few years ago over at Apple and basically assigning them to take a piece they already knew and make a story around it. It is so important to make sure your audience has a good story to tell about your magic. It occurred to me that the best stories are the ones where they are involved.

I was doing Crazy Man's Handcuffs with a story about freedom. We all think we are free, but we give away our freedom. We go to school, and we have given away 3 hours, then 6 hours a day. Then we go to college, and it is not only the class time, it is the work. Then we get a job, we get married, and we get a mortgage. We give away all that freedom that we think we have. But we can take it back—and then the bands come apart. But the good part is when I get them to tell me their own experience giving away their freedom, and have them hold the band, and I say, "Yeah, but you have the option to take it back. Say the words 'I am free,' and pull". That moment when their rubber band passes through mine, that is a powerful moment, and creates a story that they will tell. If they just watched the story, it is a different, less powerful experience.

TOBIAS: (Noticing Doug's attire) I am guessing that you are dressed for the conversation on costumes.

Wired for Wonder

DOUGLAS: I am a magician, so when I go to work, I put on bright clothes. This would be something I would wear to the street. I would probably add something like a fancy vest. I mentioned sound, movement, and color, and costuming is certainly a part of that. This is a nice bright blue vest, and I put a nice pocket scarf in it.

TOBIAS: Very nice.

DOUGLAS: And a bright fedora usually.

I believe that buskers can wear whatever they would like to and be successful. I have seen everything succeed. But I also firmly believe that if you are doing it for a living, you get paid more if you look like you are worth more. So, dressing nicely attracts more money.

TOBIAS: And more attention. People pay less attention if you are just like everybody else.

DOUGLAS: For sure. It is much more challenging to rely solely on your charisma. It is possible. I have seen all kinds. I have seen shirtless magicians work. Bums who can barely do a card trick succeed just because they are confident. But the costuming is an important element for stopping the crowd.

TOBIAS: It would be different in different kinds of magic theater. For example, if you are on the stage portraying the elegant gentleman from the Gilded Age, you are on the stage, so you already have the attention, and now you can put your costume efforts into creating character. We talked a little bit about music and amplification. I am not sure what prompts me to come back to that, but is there a particular kind of music you like to use?

DOUGLAS: I do not use music in my show, but I know something like 90% of the bigger acts do. It is an important part. Look at that trilogy: sound, movement, and color. You have that sound playing at the beginning, and what do you play? You play tunes that people are familiar with. So they hear and think, "Oh, that is my favorite. I like that song". And they look where it is coming from, and now we have this guy in a colorful outfit moving around. And then, "Come on folks, it is showtime!".

Chapter 1: Varieties of Magic Theater

If you are amplified, that also contributes as part of that trilogy, because your voice is now commanding your audience, and that is not to be overlooked as part of the sound factor. I have seen magicians work silently, completely silent, to music only. This is a great way to approach the street. It certainly helps if you are working international venues—and if you are a busker, it is likely that you will be, because it requires travel if you are professional on the road. Some people do find a sweet spot to stay year round, but most of the time, you are going to be out of town three or four months a year.

TOBIAS: I have seen some performers who speak, but they do not speak in a particular language. They go, "Hey, yo!" with grunts and laughs—things audiences can understand no matter where they come from.

DOUGLAS: There was a wonderful artist who worked in New Orleans, Perry the Hobo. He was a clown and he did balloons, but he also did a lot of magic. He did some thumb tip work. He would do the bra trick—which actually worked for him because he is a hobo clown, a street clown in New Orleans. He smoked and had a beer in his hand most of the time. But my point is his sound was a whistle. He had mastered the art of whistling and he could communicate with his audience through that sound.

TOBIAS: I would like to see that.

DOUGLAS: His students would pick up the bird warbler — checkers who just did balloons but did it in a theatrical way. He would command an entire audience just by making these balloons. He would dress a kid up in the middle, but his communication was all through the bird warbler.

TOBIAS: I understand. I know Jeff McBride loves using the squeaker.

DOUGLAS: Great example.

TOBIAS: Like from a stuffed animal, but you put it in your mouth and suddenly you are a character.

DOUGLAS: You take that act on the street, it kills.

37

Wired for Wonder

TOBIAS: I always think part of Jeff's secret is that he *did* work on the street. He was a student of Jeff Sheridan.

DOUGLAS: I am sure he was influenced by Jeff Sheridan. Did he actually work the streets then?

TOBIAS: Yes, not a lot, but I think down on Washington Square and on the streets. He worked for a while with some street break dancers where he would perform. He would pop and lock with them, and then he would step out and do magic.

DOUGLAS: And magic can really be the best highlight for a dance show. You get better fast because you get those repetitions. I had no idea that was part of his history, but no wonder he got so good so young. That makes sense now.

TOBIAS: Exactly. And it was partly the 24/7 magician thing, which he still preaches. Jeff is always on. I stayed at his house for a while. You go downstairs after sleeping for three hours, and it is 2 o'clock in the morning. Jeff is in the living room, practicing. I ask, "When do you sleep?". But when I first knew him, he was doing Club Ibis and Mostly Magic and Triple Inn late at night, almost every day. So he would do his first magic, probably working with Jeff Sheridan in the park in the afternoons, then full bore from 6:00 PM until 3:00 AM, and then he would go home and sleep. He was part of the whole New York magic scene. When you are not on the street performing, you are at Tannen's trading secrets and hanging with other magicians.

I have young magicians ask all the time, "What does it take to become a Jeff McBride or a Marco Tempest?". I tell them you have to love it so much that you do not take time out to sleep.

DOUGLAS: That is right.

TOBIAS: At that point, you are getting in that 10 thousand hours. It is like Mozart—the 10,000 hour thing where that is how you reach mastery. You say, "Yes, but some people are just talented. What about Mozart? A genius at the age of 12". But it turns out his dad was a piano teacher, and he had his 10,000 hours in on the piano by the time he was 12. The talent is in loving it enough to do it.

Chapter 1: Varieties of Magic Theater

DOUGLAS: And all too often, magicians do not realize how hard it is to do it well. They have a presumption that learning a self-working trick is half the battle. They think the trick itself is the thing.

TOBIAS: Exactly. One of the things that really struck me about our conversation last week was the idea that you must command.

DOUGLAS: You do not ask them if they want something. You do not do that.

TOBIAS: How did you learn to do that? Did it come naturally to you? Did you fail a lot?

DOUGLAS: Not at all. I think that perception of what to do out there came from watching so many new street performers struggle on the street by not doing that. They will say, "Doug, what can I do to make this better?". And I see the major fault. When people ask me about street performing now, that is certainly one of the first pieces of advice I tell them: "Command your audience with complete confidence. Tell them what you want them to do and what you expect. Tell them what to expect from you as well". It is important to convey the structure of the show. "Hey folks, I am going to do this, and you are going to see this, and then this is going to happen, and everyone is going to get excited".

TOBIAS: Certainly.

DOUGLAS: That helps you command their attention, too.

TOBIAS: Absolutely. I know one of the things for restaurant magicians is that part of your purpose for being there is to get the gig that these people might be hosting at another time. Every gig should lead to another. Do you find any of that on the street or is there no time for it?

DOUGLAS: For me, it is rare, but it does happen. I would not suggest it as a business model for street performers. But then again, maybe if it was approached in a more businesslike way. Generally buskers are out there because they are not businesslike. A lot of us enjoy being free and not having to worry about showing up at 8 o'clock at wherever a gig is going to be. But if you handed out cards and had a nice sign that said, "Hire me here," that is going to move your needle on some level. Smart marketing can probably make a difference in income.

TOBIAS: Yes, I would think so. I could see how it might hurt you, too, by cutting into your immediate take.

DOUGLAS: You pick your battles. I would say it also depends on where you are busking. If you are in a tourist-centric area like New Orleans, you are probably not going to book as many gigs. If you are working a hometown event, though, like if you are at a fair or festival in your environment where locals will see you, that is different.

TOBIAS: I would think that your central purpose is a little bit against it, too. I talked, in the chapter about restaurant magic, about Eugene Burger used to turn down tips. He said, "If they give me $20, they think of me as a $20 magician. I want them to think of me as a $2500 magician for their party. So I tell them, 'Thank you. They pay me very well here, but if you want to hire me on Saturday night at the country club, I am available'".

DOUGLAS: On that note, I think the perceived buyer is going to think your rate should be lower because you are on the street. But the truth is, these guys on the street are making $1,000 a day doing what they want, when they want to do it. They might not care about your gig, most of the time.

TOBIAS: Have you been approached, based on your street performance, to do trade shows? In my mind, there are a lot of similarities based on your ability to attract and keep an audience.

DOUGLAS: Here is a fun story. When I first started in Chicago, I was 18, performing in front of the Hancock Tower or the Sears Tower. A businessman snatched me up and said, "Come with me to my sales meeting". He took me to the top of the Hancock Tower to perform for his little group there. I did a show. The guy tipped me well and said to the group, "Now Doug is a busker. You all tip him good". I passed the hat there in the Sears Tower for a group of business people. It was nice. I was out there working, 18, 19 and new. To bag $100

Chapter 1: Varieties of Magic Theater

from these businessmen in the 80s was a pretty good hit for a lunchtime show.

TOBIAS: Exactly. And it shows that there are people like that who respect you for being out there and doing that. They get it.

DOUGLAS: Let me read you an email that I received yesterday. This is a good example of things that happen. Subject: Talking to my group. "Hi Doug, I am Rich Lang. Reaching out to see if you would be interested in talking with a group I am part of. We are all private event DJs and event producers. We meet each year to learn from each other. I had the idea of having a session called 'What We Can Learn and Steal from a Street Performance'. You know, what skills and methodology can an experienced busker teach us about performing for a group?".

These are entertainment professionals seeing how buskers have talents and skill sets that could apply to them and reaching out to me for that kind of talk.

TOBIAS: I actually reached the point, when I was managing acts, that if you could perform on the street, I was interested in you. If you had never done that, maybe not. You might not have what it takes to capture an audience's attention, and you might be a wonderful artist, but it was going to be a lot harder to sell you in the corporate market and other venues. What would you tell somebody who was just starting in magic to encourage them to get out on the street?

DOUGLAS: I tell them all the time that the most important thing to become a good magician is to perform as much as possible. With street performing, and I tell them this, it does not have to be about the money. It can just be about getting better and sharing your art with the public. Everyone thinks street performing equals passing the hat. But what if you do not even make that part of the equation? You are going to be more confident in commanding your audience because you do not have to worry about that factor.

So, I tell students that. I say, "Go find yourself a spot where you can get out there and do your shows and get your flight time in, and develop audience rapport and start building a

Wired for Wonder

theatrical experience". How do you know where to start? Where do you go? It is hard to get good feedback when you are doing family shows. You are entertaining, trying things out for your mom or dad or school friends. That is a hard audience on the street. It is hard to get invited for other gigs until you know what you are going to learn from that hard audience.

TOBIAS: And, honestly, the street is the only place you can just go out and do it.

DOUGLAS: Restaurants, as you mentioned, can be a good option, but street performing is ready today. Unless your town has an ordinance against it, and if they do, it is probably illegal and you should just go do it anyway and let them take you to court. The motto is, "Ask for forgiveness, not permission"—that is the buskers' credo.

TOBIAS: I found out that first came from a woman, Grace Hopper. She was one of the first programmers on the UNIVAC way back in the 1950s. She was the same woman who coined the term "a bug" for when a program has a problem, because the original computer bug was actually a cockroach. The UNIVAC took up a whole room, and one day the machine just was not working. They searched and searched, and finally found that cockroach that had crawled in and caused a short circuit. After that, when a computer program has a problem, we say, "There is a bug in it". But she was the one—a navy officer—who told her team "ask forgiveness not permission" because they often did not have time to clear things through the chain of command. So I think it is perfect for street performers because, how bad can the punishment be—they will maybe fine you $50, but usually they will give you a warning and say, "Go".

DOUGLAS: I was arrested in New Orleans for street performing. I actually spent the night in Orleans Parish Prison. I did break a law about performing after 8:00 PM on Bourbon Street. The policeman approached me and said, "Young man, do you know what time it is?". I said, "No, sir". And he said, "It is time to get a watch. It is 8:02. Come with me". And down to the pokey I went. So, it can happen. It is a freedom, though. As long as you are not obstructing the

Chapter 1: Varieties of Magic Theater

public thoroughfare, you can go out there and show your art. In all the court cases that I am familiar with where street performers have had to go to bat for themselves, they win. Sometimes it is a process to get lawyers and go to court dates, and it sucks. But at the end of it, the court ultimately has to go, "Yes, he was just out there expressing his art".

TOBIAS: Yes. Today, you can almost always just go to the city hall web page and search for ordinances about street performing. Or just walk in, in person, and ask someone if you are not in a huge city.

DOUGLAS: Yes, we are in a wonderful 'age of information' where you can do that. I have some notes on street performing, and that is what I recommend. Go look it up online.

TOBIAS: Yes, which reminds me—for people interested in street performing, what are some good sources? Where would you send them? Pamphlets, websites, where can they learn?

DOUGLAS: Right now, today for free, I would say go to Jimmy Talks-a-Lot Substack. Jimmy is a buddy of mine. He has been busking for almost 30 years. He published a blog in the early 2000s, and about four years ago, he started a Substack where he writes all the time. There is a college level course in busking for free, and then he does have a membership offer, and you can offer support in written form.

Real Magic Magazine. Cosmo is a legendary busker, and he has published an enormous amount of street performing content, including *The Art of Street Performing* featuring Cellini. It is a three-volume series. You will see Cellini work and some of his students. Cellini does a full breakdown on many of the things I am talking about today—sound, movement, color, all of that. So, five bucks a month for *Real Magic Magazine*; you can get into that content and a lot of other busking stuff. And while I am speaking of Cosmo, I always recommend his DVD set, *Tales from the Street.* That is, I think, some of the most concise information for smaller style sleight-of-hand shows.

TOBIAS: Fantastic. None of that is stuff I had encountered.

DOUGLAS: And one more: that is Cellini's book, *The Royal Touch.* I think that is the best book for both effects and information. It is also one of the most beautiful magic books you will ever open. So, there is a book, there is an online video resource, and written blog information. Free, cheap—and you are going to have to hunt for Cellini's book if you want it.

One more: There is a wonderful book. Cellini's love interest from the 80s and 90s wrote a book called *No Ordinary Magic*, and it is her viewpoint of traveling the world with Cellini as the girlfriend and student of a street performer. This is a wonderful look at what the lifestyle is like through the eyes of someone close to, but not in the middle of it all. So, check that one, too.

The Magic Castle

There's no place like The Magic Castle! Dedicated wholly to the art of performing magic, it is at once a clubhouse, replete with library, private lectures, lots of special members' privileges and more—and it's also a showcase for magic in all its forms. Non-magician members bring friends, and it's a very special treat to be invited for dinner and shows at "The Castle." Even in 2025, they maintain a strict dress code.

From intimate close-up magic in the Close-up Gallery, to the slightly larger Parlour of Prestidigitation, the stage shows in The Palace of Mystery, a special brand of bar magic in the Library Bar, or the slightly off-beat presentations in the Peller Theater, visitors are provided the opportunity to witness the very best current magical artists available for nearly every form of performing magic.

The Magic Castle is the creation of two brothers, Bill and Mitch Larsen, both passionate and talented performers. To this day, it bears the imprint of their personalities. It is also the home of The Academy of Magical Arts—the magic world's equivalent of the Academy of Motion Pictures, creator of the Academy Awards. Each year, magicians from around the world vie to perform at the Castle and make themselves eligible for one of the magical Academy Awards. Only the best are invited, and once someone has "played the Castle," the credit goes into all their press materials.

Chapter 1: Varieties of Magic Theater

Because the Magic Castle is primarily a club for magicians and fans of magic, it is unique in terms of both the performances given and the purpose of those performances. For performers, a performance at the Castle is as much a quest for approval from your colleagues as it is for the audience who attend. One accepts an engagement there, often at a lower fee than one might earn elsewhere, as much for the opportunity to spend the week with esteemed colleagues and to add the prestigious engagement to your resumé as for any other reason.

Corporate/Industrial Shows

People who call themselves corporate magicians are actually a varied lot, ranging from those who stroll at cocktail parties, to those who gather crowds at tradeshow booths. Some others appear several times during a large corporation's "general session" events, creating the sense of a through line and style for the event, and waking the thousands of attendees up in between the endless executive talks. Still others help create and perform at special "product launch" events when a big company is launching a new product — a new model of their top line automobile, for example. Some (like yours truly) combine magic with a keynote talk designed to help a particular crowd think in different, more empowering ways about their work.

General Session Featured Performer

Working as manager/producer for both Marco Tempest and Jeff McBride, our best jobs were being hired to perform as part of a large "general session" event. Huge companies like Pfizer or Hewlett-Packard would ship thousands of their top employees to Las Vegas, Orlando, or some other resort location, and put on events that lasted several days. Attendees might be treated to Vegas shows in the evening, but had to be up and in the venue—which could be as small as a ballroom or as large as a sports stadium—bright and early the next morning.

Energetic, rock-anthem-style music would usually play as the attendees found their way to their seats, where they were going to be for the next four or five hours. Lights would scan across the audience,

Wired for Wonder

and motivational company videos would be shown on the giant screens surrounding them. At some point, everyone was seated, and the room lights went down. Typically, that's when Marco Tempest's first performance would start. A digital countdown would appear on all the screens, and an explosion of light and cloud of smoke would flash as it hit zero. Marco would appear in silhouette, walk up to the big screen, and pluck out the bright light. He would pass it through his body once or twice, then hurl it out into the audience, where it would circle over their heads, then return to him on stage. He would take it back and hurl it into the giant screen, where it would flash again... and a silhouette would appear on the screen. A mysterious figure, who would walk to the edge of the screen and out onto the stage with a spark of light on his shoulder. Typically, this was the company CEO, and he would receive a thunderous round of applause as he took the spark of light off his shoulder and handed it to Marco as he exited.

"A big round of applause for my friend, Marco Tempest. He'll be back later!"

Then the CEO would talk for 40 minutes or more before Marco came back for another performance segment. We used to joke that we got hired to add style and wake people up at regular intervals, in between boring speeches.

Marco had several unique talents that made this kind of corporate performance a key part of his career. First, he had a deep sense of style. When Marco and his team produced a bit of video for a corporation, it carried the look and feel of the corporation's internally produced materials, but looked as though a master stylist had taken it and moved it to the next level. He made them look better!

He also had a great sense of how to work in spectacular elements that were relatively inexpensive to produce and transport. A flying light was just a super-bright LED on the end of a roll of fishing line. The huge, amazing graphics usually appeared on the same giant screens as the rest of the event's PowerPoints and other materials. We delivered digital files. Marco often traveled with his own smallish flat-screen

Chapter 1: Varieties of Magic Theater

monitor on a stand. This was tricked out to make it easy for him to create the illusion of things going in and out of the screen. A brilliant light would go in, Marco's hands would appear to go in and manipulate the light into something... oh, the company's logo! So we could customize each and every piece he performed, mostly just by changing the video component. Clients were left feeling that we had created the whole thing just for them.

When creating performances for this kind of client, it is especially important to make them feel, as Marco did, that they are receiving a unique, one-time-only event customized by you and your team to their particular needs. Performers who specialize in this kind of show are few and far between. Most who work this market simply do a standard show they've developed with a couple of banners showing a company logo. That's fine, and might keep you working if you have several event producers who like you and your work. But if you want to earn top dollar in this market, learn to create special material that can appear to be customized from beginning to end for each event.

Also, be aware of the environment you will be working in. Chances are that you and your team will arrive at the venue 24 hours before your performance. You will have made arrangements so that your lighting and sound cues have reached the tech crews weeks before the event, and the sound and video files will be loaded before you arrive. You'll have a very short time to set up your equipment, check sound, video, and whatever else is necessary for the performance. If you're lucky, you'll get a full technical run-through... after which your producer may request a few changes. The morning of the event, you and the technical crew will arrive at 4:00 or 5:00 AM for the performance that is to begin at 7:00 AM. You can do a final check of any items that have been changed. You might get five minutes with the CEO or other speakers to rehearse their entries and exits as they will interact with you... and then you go on!

The miracle of all of this is possible because you will be working with some of the best technicians in the business. These people produce 50 or 60 events like the one where you will be performing every year. If you can match their level of excellence and professionalism, every show will go off without a hitch. This was a huge surprise for me, as my previous work had been in Broadway theater, where we rehearsed in a studio for three weeks, and then had a week or more developing and rehearsing the show with full sound, lights, and moving stage sets. Doing the whole process in just a few hours, and having it come off nearly perfectly every time still amazes me. It was also a fun challenge for Marco and me (usually his only on-site team member).

Keynote Speaker

I've seen many keynote speeches by famous corporate speakers. Some are highly emotional and motivational - a former football star who lost his legs in an accident and went on to become a US senator, talking about his struggle, for example. Others are famous visionaries like Ray Kurzweil, or popular financial experts like Faith Popcorn. (Look them up if you don't know them already).

My friend Paul Draper does keynote speaking with magic. He is a trained cultural anthropologist, mentalist and magician. An all around showman who (almost) always dresses in a three-piece suit and carries an air of good humored professionalism with him everywhere. Paul delivers talks specially created for his various clients — but actually, there are only about three things he gets hired to talk about.

One is how to build a better culture within a company. We call that the "team-building" talk. It has certain elements that never really change. But Paul learns about the group he is delivering the talk for, and weaves in examples from their recent experience, the names of leaders within the company, and actually involves members from the audience. The result is that the talk feels like it has been fully created and customized for that group.

Another popular subject for corporate talks is "innovation and disruption." Companies, especially new ones, succeed by disrupting markets. Think of Uber disrupting the taxi markets around the world,

Chapter 1: Varieties of Magic Theater

for example, by applying a new business model for ways to hail a ride. So companies want to train their executives to be more creative, to take bigger chances, and to have the courage to create disruption in the market they serve. Paul has a number of great stories and performance magic pieces about innovation and creativity.

Many times, a corporate event will be a kind of celebration of the company's recent successes. "We sold more than anyone! We brought new innovative products to market and destroyed our competition!" Whatever. In these situations, the ideal keynote speakers are those who talk about sales, negotiation, and other business related skills. If you have a great talk teaching those things, there's a lot of work out there for you! Spicing the talk up with a few magic tricks will set you apart from the pack.

Here's a secret Paul told me recently. Sometimes he'll get to an event where he is hired to speak — usually because one of the top executives at the company saw one of his shows and loved it — and an hour before the show he'll be chatting with that executive and/or the event producer, and he'll say, "Wow, you have some great speakers here already. Do you really want me to do the keynote we talked about (on company culture, or sales, or whatever) — or would it be better if I just did my 30 minutes as a show of mental magic? Something to lighten the mood." Their answer is often, "Oh, the show would really probably be better. Can you do that?" And of course he can. Always be prepared!

Another thing to remember, if you want to pursue this kind of work, is that magic is that special kind of participatory event, unlike other kinds of theater. Take advantage of that, and get your audience involved. Make them chant, stand, wave their hands in the air. Get key executives from the company to be your volunteers onstage. If you just let the audience sit and watch, you're missing out on the things that set magicians apart from other keynote speakers.

Trade Show Performer

Wired for Wonder

Trade show magic is another unique situation. Here, the best performer doesn't always win. Your job is primarily to draw audiences to the trade show booth, secondarily to make their product seem attractive, and finally to help "qualify" possible customers and get them to talk to one of the company representatives in the booth. In many ways, trade show performers are like street performers, but with higher price tags and more exacting requirements.

The upside: these jobs generally pay very well. Upwards of $2,000 per day plus expenses. The downside: a typical trade show day goes from 7:00 or 8:00 AM until at least 5:00 PM, and you'll often be doing shows once every 20 or 30 minutes. It's exhausting work. For those who become really good at providing what exhibitors need, though, performing at trade shows can be immensely rewarding.

Your setting will be in front of (or within) a booth on a trade show floor. Ideally, you'll be on a small stage that puts you above your potential audience, so if they are two or three rows back, they can still see you. You'll have some kind of amplification for your voice or music to help attract attention, but not so much that you'll annoy the booths on either side of you or across the aisle. The story you tell will be about the company who hired you and their products. Your success will depend on how many people you can get that story across to in a way that results in sales in the booth.

As for your audience, well, they've chosen to attend the trade show, or are being paid to be there. Many of them are potential buyers, usually for their own companies. Trade shows are ways for potential customers, usually businesses themselves, to meet potential suppliers. Macy's Department Store chain will have buyers for clothing, housewares, jewelry, etc. The distributors and manufacturers at trade shows they attend will be fashion brands, clothing manufacturers, housewares brands, jewelry and fragrance brands, and more. Your job as performer at these shows is to get their attention and help them make connections.

Strolling at After Party Events

Chapter 1: Varieties of Magic Theater

Many corporate events, from those big general sessions that go on for days to trade shows, which also go on for days, will supply their attendees with evening parties and other events. Magicians are often hired to spice up those events. Strolling at a big party, whether it is sponsored by a business or a private individual, is very different from performing on a stage.

Often at these events, the magician's role is that of "icebreaker." You are providing quick bits of something interesting for groups who may not know each other well so that they have something interesting to talk about. If you can use your performance to get them to say their names, that helps them get to know one another better. Magicians who let their ego take over and spend most of the party with one particularly responsive group might feel they had a wonderful, successful evening—but the person who hired them feels like they've failed to do what they were hired for, which is to meet, introduce, and entertain as many of the guests as possible.

This is also one of those situations where the performer has very little control over the environment. There may be loud music, making it difficult for you to speak and be heard. People may be drunk, or on their best behavior. The crowd might be made up of groups of old friends who haven't seen each other for a long time and don't appreciate you interrupting their conversations. The room might be brightly lit, or be mostly dark. You can learn about some of these things by visiting the space with your host before the party, or by having discussions where you ask about them beforehand, but, perhaps more than any other form of magic, you must be prepared to be flexible. A good party magician might only perform four or five pieces, repeated again and again throughout the evening—but you probably need to be prepared with different sets of four or five that will suit different situations you might encounter.

I seldom actually perform magic, preferring to be in the "behind the scenes" mode, helping to make my clients stand out. However, I was once asked to stand in for a friend who found himself suddenly double-booked. It was for a high-end Christmas party for a big San

Wired for Wonder

Francisco tech and style industry company, and the theme was "Winter Wonderland." My friend had been booked as a kind of "Father Christmas" decked out in a white wizard's gown. He provided the costume to me, and it solved the one fear I had: how to "break in" to a group of party guests to start my performances. Because the costume was so outrageous, groups would simply come up and ask me, "Who are you? Are you a wizard? Can you do magic?" Of course I could, and did. I had so much fun playing with the groups I forgot to take the breaks that were in my contract.

Product Launch Events

Big companies, especially in the tech and pharmaceutical industries that Marco Tempest and I worked with so much, often had new products they wanted to "launch" at a special event. Sometimes these were combined with a general session, trade show, or other events, but sometimes they were just stand-alone press events. We were there to help them build a story and excitement around the new product and its launch into the market.

I particularly remember a product rollout we did for Audi, for the launch of their TT sports car back in 1999.

The company wanted to create an interesting story around the car and invited dealers from all over the world for a three-day event at Universal Studios, first in California, and then in Orlando, Florida. I'm guessing there were at least 400 dealers in each group. They were treated to special dinners, golfing, free days at the theme parks, and more. But the highlight of the event was to be the rollout of the car, and creating the show around that was our job.

The basic "plot" of the show was that, at the last minute, the company had run into problems and was unable to actually deliver the prototype for the launch. It would be ready in a few days, but we could give one lucky dealer the experience of driving one using virtual reality.

Virtual reality was a new thing back in the late 1990s. A few game installations had appeared in a few arcades, but it was mostly used in

Chapter 1: Varieties of Magic Theater

simulators to train pilots and as part of some of the newer "rides" at theme parks like Universal. So the idea that someone could actually walk into a virtual world was still novel.

This was the show we created:

A "random" brave audience member was selected to join Marco in virtual reality. He happened to have a postcard showing the new car in mock-up—something that had been given to all the attendees. Marco took his postcard and "inserted it" into a small flat screen on the stage. This activated a very large screen that filled most of the stage, and the image of the car assembled itself as a full-scale mock-up of the car.

Marco invited the audience member to "Come with me," and they walked into the side of the screen, appearing seamlessly in the virtual environment with the car. They walked around the car, admiring it, and Marco suggested... "Let's take it for a drive."

We saw them get into the car, start it up, and take it for a wild ride through various real and mocked-up, video game–style scenes. Suddenly lights began to flash, smoke billowed from behind the screen. We saw the two of them throw open the doors of the car and make their way to the edge of the screen and back out onto the stage, just as the entire auditorium went dark, just for a second or two. The image of the car was still on the screen, but now in a lit-up wireframe mode. It flashed several times, then "went off" in a shower of sparks... and when the smoke cleared, there was the real Audi TT sitting center stage exactly where the screen had been.

Dealers were invited to the stage to examine the new car, get in and out, and then out to a nearby racetrack the next day to actually drive the new car.

Our job, to create this experience, was, first, to help the marketing team from Audi create the script. Then we designed a stage and screen setup in which we could actually deliver the experience. Marco and his video team then went to work filming the "volunteer" and building the

53

onscreen experience. Meanwhile, I had a team of illusion and electronics designers working to build a black covering for the car with the wireframe light strips embedded, and the framework we would use to snatch it off the car when the smoke and sparks went off. That bit of pyro was handled by the team from Universal, working to our specifications.

This is the level of production you need to be able to deliver if you really want to work at the top of this kind of corporate theater. First, you need the vision to create and sell the idea for the show. Then the expertise to find and work with all the various teams who will help you deliver your show. Finally, you'll need to have good people skills to make everything and everyone work together to deliver the experience seamlessly. For the audience, it needs to seem to just happen.

An event like this Audi launch probably cost Audi upwards of $1 million for each of the two locations, not including the show we put on, which was by no means inexpensive. It's fun to work at the high end, if you can handle the pressure and deliver on that level. It's definitely not for everyone, though.

Workshop Breakouts

I worked corporate events for years before I understood that magician/speakers could also work the "breakout" sessions that typically happen after that big morning "general session." The large group breaks into smaller groups and receives training in the new product, or in better techniques for selling, or actually does the team-building exercises talked about during the general session. If you have the expertise a company is looking for, and can lead this kind of session, you can double your income for a particular corporate event. But remember, this event isn't a show. It's a workshop.

Can you weave what you teach in your keynote—on innovation, culture, team building, sales, whatever—into a life-changing, hands-on training session? If so, go for it!

Chapter 1: Varieties of Magic Theater

Cruise Ships

Since I started working in the magic business, cruise ships have proliferated like rabbits! There were always a few performers who specialized in working cruise ships, but they were not widely known. This was partly by choice, because those who were good at it could work most of the year on cruises, and there weren't that many gigs, so they didn't want to encourage competition. The other big reason they weren't well-known, though, was that they were always at sea, and back then if you were at sea, it meant you were out of touch with most of the rest of the world. Today things are different— with social media, satellite internet and more, cruise ship performers can become quite well-known.

As with other forms of magical theater, the cruise ship has specific requirements. Your boss is the Cruise Director, and they will have very specific ideas of "what works" and what doesn't for their particular audiences. An audience on one of Holland America's World Cruises is very different from one on a Disney or Carnival Cruise. The Cruise Director will insist that performers do NOTHING that might offend anyone in their audiences. This means costuming that's not too risqué, and material that has no "blue" overtones. Material that refers to the cruise experience is encouraged.

Every cruise line is different, but it's important to remember, as the performer, that even though you might only be performing for two nights each week, you are always "on," as a representative of the cruise line. Behavior must, at all times, be within their guidelines. I know of more than one performer permanently banned — not for their performances, but for getting drunk and behaving badly during their off hours.

So, as with most venues and settings, it's important to remember what your purpose is, and why you've been hired. If you're interested in pursuing this, it will pay you handsomely to make friends with those who have succeeded in the business, and learn as much as you can from them!

Wired for Wonder

Just a Sliver

Eugene Burger used to love to tell us, "There are many rooms in the House of Magic," and now we've visited just a few of those rooms - each offering possibilities to create theater with our magic. Looking back over this particular group, you'll notice that each one serves a somewhat different purpose, providing a different set of benefits for those who hire the magician, as well as for the audiences who see them. As a strolling magician at a cocktail party, your performance might serve as an ice-breaker — something to introduce different party-goers to one another and give them something interesting to talk about. At a trade show booth, your primary job is to attract attention and bring people to your booth. The best trade show performers also enhance their client's products, help to qualify sales leads, and more. In a casino, the magic show is there partly to encourage you to come to that casino instead of one of its competitors, to get them into an excited state, and then back out onto the casino floor to gamble before the excitement wears off. At a kid's birthday party, the magic show is partly to attract friends to come and experience the novelty, partly to keep the kids occupied, and partly to make the host and the kid with the birthday seem like heroes to their friends.

Each of these types of magical performance takes place in different kinds of venues, requires different size effects to be performed, and requires different kinds of stories to be told with the magic. Is it just to attract attention and keep them engaged with the novelty of the performance (street performer), or is it to make party goers feel more comfortable interacting and giving them topics to discuss? Is the magician's character "larger than life," like Siegfried and Roy, or "just like one of us," as when magicians are hired to perform strolling magic at a corporate cocktail party?

The big lesson here? Know what sort of magical theater you are offering. Figure out 'what it's for,' and what theatrical tools you'll have in order to achieve the goals of that particular kind of magic. We'll be looking at some of those tools in the next section.

Chapter 2
What Makes a Good Story

Because I spent so many years working with Jeff McBride at his Magic & Mystery School, I've encountered hundreds of magicians who insist that, "I'm not a story-telling magician." What they mean is that they don't "tell stories," per se. The truth is it's impossible to perform without your audience experiencing a story. Even a circus act like a juggler leaves audiences with stories to tell. "First he juggled three balls, and then three bowling pins. He moved on to 4 bowling pins, and told us he had never been able to do 5, but that he would try, just for us today. At first he couldn't do it, but then he did! And his partner threw another pin at him and all of a sudden he was doing the impossible, juggling 6 pins! And we were there to see it!"

That juggler didn't tell a story, except to say that he didn't think he could do 5 pins... but the audience came away with a great story. Psychologists and others who study our minds tell us that stories are how we make sense of our world. Until you can tell someone what happened to you, that thing isn't real for you or for them. So... learn to create good stories for your audiences if you want to succeed. Learn to tell those stories well even if you never open your mouth on stage.

Another way to think of this is that your performance is creating a memory. The better the story, the better the memory.

Character Drives Story

According to Aristotle in his Poetics, a good story has a protagonist and an antagonist. In classical latin, an "agon" is a struggle or a battle. An agonist is a warrior. So we have a hero fighting his enemy. The protagonist has a big goal, and the antagonist(s) are there to make it difficult for the protagonist to reach that goal. All great stories are about conflict and struggle.

Recently, reading about what makes a good screenplay, I discovered that there is always a third character, or at least a third role, in every story: the victim. The victim, and how they are affected, gives stories their scope. It's why we care. Sometimes either the antagonist or protagonist is also the victim, but often there is a third character. A person whose life will be even more strongly affected than the two warriors by the outcome of their battle.

On a podcast for screenwriters, one of the more successful ones commented, "I don't get why people make such a big deal about how to create a character. A character is created by what they want most, and what they are willing to do to get it." That may be an oversimplification, but it gives a great insight into what it takes to build a character and story — especially a dramatic one.

There is one additional thing we need to know about our main character, and that's whatever it is within themselves that's holding them back from getting the thing they want so badly. This, the thing that holds them back and that they must conquer before they can have the thing they desire — that is the theme of your story, and where the true story lies, if it's a good one.

That said, building and performing characters with quirky traits is fun. Using different voices, rhythms, postures and more can go a long way to spicing up your performances. We'll cover this in more detail when we get to the chapter on acting for magicians.

Here's another thing you might want to consider when creating characters for your magical story: The audience wants to identify with and root for the hero. If you can keep that in mind when creating that character, it will help you create more successful stories. I've seen magicians create stories and encourage an audience to cheer the hero and boo the antagonist. This can be a favorite at family parties and others for young audience, but adults love it, too.

Chapter 2: What Makes a Good Story

Plot

We speak of plot when we're describing (or acting out) the actions the characters take, which are based on their conflicting desires. Plot is what happens in the story. Something happens, which causes something else to happen, which causes something else...

Going back to Aristotle, we find there are five main parts of a plot: Exposition, Rising Action, Crisis, Climax, and Denouement. Understanding these can help you create better plots.

Exposition is where we give the audience what they need to know about the world they are entering. Many films begin with a moving long shot, perhaps flying over countryside till we see what appears to be a medieval village, ultimately landing in a farmyard at the edge of the village. There is a maid milking a goat, and a young man hanging on a fence nearby chatting with her. While there is not as yet any conflict, we have the information we need to understand where and when the story will take place, and have probably met the two main characters, whose interaction rapidly lays out the bones of the story to follow. That's Exposition.

Here's something Aristotle didn't tell us: Part of the Exposition portion of a story is the moment the audience enters what I call "story space." You've experienced this. Suddenly, in your mind, the real world falls away and you feel like you are in the environment of the story, perhaps even experiencing it as though you have become the main character. This is an important part of why we have exposition, and as a storyteller, an important part of your job. Ideally, you draw them into the story space and don't let them go until it's over, and they can go "live happily ever after."

At some point, someone lets us know they are trying to get or achieve something, but feels there is too much in the way. Someone else discourages them, or otherwise provides barriers that prevent them from moving forward. The protagonist tries to overcome those barriers. Then other barriers arise and need to be overcome. This is Rising Action.

At some point, the skirmishes come to a head. We reach a point where the protagonist will either get the thing they really desire or be thwarted, and their antagonist wins. Sometimes a story will have several of these Crisis moments where we think the protagonist has won, or lost, but then discover they really haven't, but they can find a way to recover. In any case, the Crisis is a turning point.

Finally we reach the Climax of our story, which is the moment our hero actually does win or lose the thing they've been striving for. More than that—the climax is the moment the hero transcends the thing that was holding them back. This is the moment of real growth, real transcendence, and the reason all great stories are a bit magical.

Finally, there is the Denouement, the wrap-up. At this point, all of the subplots get wrapped up, and there is an event—often a wedding or a funeral—which sums up what has happened. At this point, if we (and the protagonist) haven't already realized it, we come to an understanding of what the hero learned, of what it was all about. "And the moral of the story is..." or "And they all lived happily ever after."

Screenwriters often talk about a three-act structure, in which the first act is the "setup," where we get to know the characters, the place and time, and the central conflict is defined. Act two is the struggle, the rising action, crisis, reversals, etc. Act three is the resolution—climax and denouement.

These are useful ways of thinking about story, but shouldn't be seen as rigid structures. Everything is connected, and can be woven in different ways for different emotional impact. Mysteries often withhold key elements that would normally be laid out in exposition or setup, so that they can provide a surprise or shock when they are revealed, just as one example.

Chapter 2: What Makes a Good Story

The thing to remember when developing the story for your piece of magic is that conflict is your friend. Sure, you can go through the steps of your trick with just an explanation of what you're doing. "First, I lay out these five cards. Then I..." But the story remembered will be a boring one, if your performance is remembered at all.

Make the props represent characters, or make them belong to characters, and make sure those characters want something. "The Knave of Hearts has an unbearable crush on the Queen of Spades, but the King of Spades stands in his way. His plight seems hopeless. Or does it?" Now, we, as audience, have someone and something to root for or against. Now we can feel involved. We can care about what's at stake. That makes us care about your magic!

Alternatively, we can select an audience member and assign a role to them. Hero, antagonist, victim... and now they have to be fully involved. No sitting back with arms crossed for whoever you've selected! This is a luxury seldom afforded to performers in the theater, but as magicians we can take advantage of it all the time.

Theme

I always had a difficult time understanding theme, and how it works in stories. That is, until I read a book recently by Lisa Cron, called *Wired for Story*. We've all heard that, in tragedy, our hero has a "tragic flaw." This is often a characteristic which the hero thinks gives them strength or power, but in reality causes them to fail.

In the story of Oedipus, for example, Oedipus is an unswerving moral martinet, who demands extreme adherence to the moral code he, as king, has set forth. He is a bit of a tyrant. Then he discovers that fate has placed him in a situation where, returning to his country after long absence, he has killed his own father, thinking he was a bandit on the road, and wound up marrying his mother. These are the ultimate crimes in his own philosophy, and when they are revealed to him, he puts out his own eyes and banishes himself from his kingdom — the extreme punishments he would have meted out as king to any subject discovered to have committed those crimes. Oedipus' rigidity, especially in his morals, is both his biggest strength and his greatest weakness. The entire plot of the story revolves around his first exercising that rigidity, and then about how it brings him down.

The theme of Oedipus' story: Don't be such a rigid, moral martinet!

So, the theme of your story is really the thing driving both characters and plot. In my last book, "The Performer's Edge," I teach a trick many of us learned as children. I think I learned it from the back of a cereal box. It's called "The Jumping Band." A simple effect where you place a rubber band around your index and middle fingers, make a fist, and when the fist is opened, the band has jumped to the ring and little fingers. A cute little impossibility, but hardly a great feat of magic.

My solution was to add a story. The characters in the story are Harry Houdini, a brash young American star on his first tour in Europe, where he is unknown. For publicity he wants to challenge the handcuffs used at Scotland Yard, Britain's famed crime fighters. He is sure he can get out of the cuffs, but he encounters one supercilious inspector who sees him as a brash upstart, and wants to humiliate him — and by extension, America itself. The task the inspector proposes seems truly impossible, but Houdini has to accept it because of his brash claims. So our theme is a seeming neophyte (Houdini representing America), daring the challenge the tried and true excellence of the mighty (and proud) Brit and his empire, needing to truly "do the impossible," and somehow coming away the victor. "The moral of the story is, never underestimate Houdini!"

Without a clear theme, which will usually be based on what the hero wants most and why they can't have it, stories tend not to hang together. Plots become just a string of things that happen to someone. If that someone doesn't have a running desire that they keep almost reaching, but failing because they have something they need to change about themselves before they can achieve the goal, we don't have a reason to root for them. The story lacks a through line.

Chapter 2: What Makes a Good Story

Creating Magical Stories

There are a number of ways to discover the stories we can build using our magic. One of the great things about magic tricks is that each one does have a central theme — or sometimes several possible themes.

The classical, much ridiculed, "Take a card" trick where the magician finds the card, has the theme of "That which has been lost, can often be found again." Knowing that, it becomes easier to think of stories from your own life, or from literature, in which something seems to be irretrievably lost, but is then recovered. Stories about prodigal sons, long lost family members, losing one's dignity, or a lost Bitcoin wallet can all be told using versions of this trick.

The linking rings can indicate that, "That which is separate, can be joined." Or "That which is bound together, can be separated." The rings can represent lovers who come together and drift apart, or of a young person dying to be admitted to a group, but who is continually being rejected, until one day…

The trick here is to examine the magic effect and break it down into the actions that actually happen. Describe the trick in its most basic form: "The match box is opened and closed, obviously just an ordinary, inanimate match box. But when placed on the magician's hand, it moves all by itself, stands on end and opens itself." A good trick, but not the essence. "An inanimate object suddenly moves, all by itself." That's better. "Something we think is dead, suddenly comes to life." That's kind of exciting. Any of these can become magical stories, with the magic effect itself at the center.

Another way of discovering stories for your magic is one I learned first from Jeff McBride, and then expanded on in my first book, "Beyond Deception." It consisted of making several lists. One list had five (or more) of the magical effects, the tricks, you most wanted to add to your repertory. This might include tricks like Linking Rings, card manipulation, Oil & Water… you get the idea.

Wired for Wonder

Another list was of five or more of your favorite things to do outside world of magic. You might include things like bike riding, playing your guitar, scuba diving. Activities that you really love and have had interesting experiences doing.

Another list could be your 5 favorite pieces of music. Another could be five favorite cartoon characters, or characters from fiction (Voldemort!).

Maybe you love different kinds of food, and want a list of your five favorite dishes.

Once you have your lists, take three or four of them, and place them side by side on a grid. Maybe make a spreadsheet with different columns for each list.

The object here is just to randomize and combine the lists. Could I create a version of the cups and balls as it would be performed to Beethoven's "Ode to Joy," by Bugs Bunny telling a story of his favorite adventure while surfing? Maybe there's a way to use The Professor's Nightmare to tell a story about Vito Corleone (The Godfather) encountering Sushi for the first time?

> *Creativity is just connecting things. When you ask creative people how they did something, they feel a little guilty because they didn't really do it, they just saw something. It seemed obvious to them after a while. That's because they were able to connect experiences they've had and synthesize new things. And the reason they were able to do that was that they've had more experiences or they have thought more about their experiences than other people. Unfortunately, that's too rare a commodity. A lot of people in our industry haven't had very diverse experiences. So they don't have enough dots to connect, and they end up with very linear solutions without a broad perspective on the problem. The broader one's understanding of the human experience, the better design we will have.*
>
> Steve Jobs

Chapter 2: What Makes a Good Story

Mixing and matching seemingly unrelated things is one of the keys to creativity, and a great way to avoid ever experiencing writer's block. Just take things you already love, and mix them up. Ask "what if?" Picasso asked himself, "What would the world look like if all the colors were removed except for blue?" And we got Picasso's blue period.

I think it's also important to note Steve Jobs' observation that a lot of people haven't had very diverse experiences. A broad spectrum of experiences and passions is one of the keys to creating great art, no matter what kind of artist you are. So a big part of your job is to go out and experience different kinds of activities, different cultures, different kinds of people and their stories. Magical technique is fascinating, and can become all consuming, especially for those of us not naturally social. Don't let that happen to you, unless you want to become that nerdy magician who only performs magic for other magicians.

One great way of getting out of your bubble is to join a local theater company. Most towns have a community theater, and they operate at all different levels of excellence — but they are filled with people who have a love and passion for performing in front of others. You'll make friends, begin to build that bank of experiences and stories you can lean into when you're creating your magic. You'll also learn things about being on stage, working with technicians and collaboration that might take you a lot longer to learn when operating as a lone performer.

Those are just a couple of suggestions for inspiring yourself to create magical stories using your favorite tricks. You might already have stories you find yourself telling again and again because they are particularly relevant to your own life. Find ways to enhance those stories using your magic. Whatever inspires you is likely to inspire your audiences.

Wired for Wonder

Chapter 3
The Art of Performing Magic

I suspect, if you've been performing for some time, what follows might be old news to you. However, if you're new to the stage, you should understand some of the particular jargon we use.

Directions: We determine stage directions based on what the actor, facing the audience, experiences. "Stage Right" is the actor's right, but the audience's left, because the audience is facing the stage. Sometimes we want to give directions from the audience's point of view, so we specify "House Right," which is the opposite of "Stage Right."

Once upon a time, many theaters "raked" their stages so they were higher at the back and lower close to the audience. This made it easier for some of the audience to see what was going on, especially when seated near the back of the theater. As a result, "Upstage" means toward the back of the stage, and "Downstage" means closest to the audience.

Because we use these terms "up" and "down" to mean stage directions, we don't use them when talking about things that might fly in or out from above the stage. Instead of bringing a lighting pipe down, we bring it "in," or take it "out."

Anecdote

Which brings up an interesting anecdote. In many theaters, there's a superstition that it's bad luck to whistle in the theater. The actor Yul Brynner (The King and I) was known to track down people he heard whistling and have them fired. It sounds ridiculous, doesn't it?

Wired for Wonder

But there is a reason behind the superstition. Because most of the scenery and lighting used to hang from pipes above the stage, and those pipes were controlled by hemp ropes, it was common to hire sailors to run the "flies," as the system was called. The sailors cued one another by whistling. So if someone else whistled at the wrong time, it was possible that the performers then on stage would have a large drop or pipe filled with lighting instruments suddenly drop on them. Bad luck, indeed!

In any event, the sooner you get used to using the common jargon of the stage, the easier a time you'll have working on stages everywhere. Imagine you're performing on a variety show. Before the show, the stage manager will suggest, "I'd like you to enter from stage right. You'll move downstage center, and we'll drop the main curtain in behind you." If you don't know stage right from stage left, or what the term downstage means, you'll be lost. The lighting director might tell you, "I'm going to need you to be upstage about three feet from where you are, and three feet to the left, because that's where I have this pool of light already focused." You need to know how to move according to those instructions, or you'll find yourself performing in the dark.

Performance Skills

Before we dive into the intricacies of acting and building a character, let's work a bit with the basics of becoming comfortable on stage, in front of an audience. Many people have difficulty being in front of a room with an audience watching them. They become nervous and self-conscious, and this can severely inhibit their ability to perform well.

Here's a little exercise I like to use at the beginning of a new class, whether it is for actors, magicians or speakers.

> *Let's begin becoming comfortable in front of a group with an exercise that can be done in almost any classroom or workshop situation.*
>
> *The exercise is designed to help you build your ability to give good eye contact. We'll each introduce ourselves, one-on-one with each other person in the class, while shaking hands and thus making*

Chapter 3: The Art of Performance

direct contact with that person. This will be short and direct: "Hi, I'm Tobias Beckwith, and I live right here in Las Vegas." And then the person I've just spoken to... let's say their name is Wanda: "Hi, Tobias. I'm Wanda, and I live in Santa Cruz, California. I'm pleased to meet you!" Me: "Hi, Wanda. I'm happy to meet you, too." We make a point of looking into one another's eyes as we speak and listen. The interchange is short enough that this shouldn't feel uncomfortable.

And then I go on to the next person. When I finish with that person, Wanda follows me, and we each move on to the next person, and continue until everyone has introduced themselves to everyone else. At the end of this introductory exercise, we'll each stand before the whole group, which is now acting as our audience, and Introduce ourselves at more length. "Hello. I'm Tobias, from Las Vegas. I love performing magic as part of my keynote talks for small groups. Thank you!"

I deliver each one of those sentences to a different person in my audience, making eye contact with them as I do, and taking a moment to make sure they've actually heard me before I move on to the next. I'm training myself to make sure I'm getting responses, to feel I'm part of a two-way communication and not just "talking at" my audience.

We do this exercise in order to accustom ourselves to being in front of audiences. We often feel less than comfortable with any new activity, anything we haven't done before. Everyone has different feelings about being in front of audiences, ranging from terrified to ecstatic. The only way to really become comfortable is to do it again and again.

There are, of course, some other thought techniques which can help take the edge off your terror, if you happen to be one of those who is super self-conscious and experiences stage fright. One often quoted one is to think of everyone in the audience being naked or dressed only in their underwear. While an interesting exercise, I don't find that one terribly useful.

The technique I've found works best is to have a clear purpose and idea of how you want that audience to change as a result of what you say to them. If you want to make them feel sad, happy, angry, or to laugh, and you work to make them feel those things, your internal focus is no longer on yourself. Pay attention to how you are affecting the audience, on whether you're achieving your goals, and you'll stop worrying about how you look and sound.

What is Acting?

Let's not be too pretentious here. Acting is pretending. I can't teach you to act, because you knew how, already, when you were three or four years old. Didn't you ever play at being a cowboy, or a nurse? Were you "Mommy" to your dolls? Did you dress up as some character on Halloween? If you did any of these, you were acting. However, when we think of what it means to be an actor, we usually think of something more.

According to Wikipedia, "Acting is an activity in which a story is told by means of its enactment by an actor or actress who adopts a character—in theatre, television, film, radio, or any other medium that makes use of the mimetic mode."

That "mimetic mode" is a fancy way of saying "pretending to be something else." Paintings imitate whatever the painter's subject is. Acting imitates people in action.

Konstantin Stanislavsky, a prominent Russian actor and director, defined acting as "the art of experiencing life and expressing it to an audience through the use of imagination, emotion, and intellect." According to him, an actor's task is to create a character that is authentic, believable, and emotionally engaging for the audience. He believed that actors must fully immerse themselves in the world of the character(s) they play, understanding their thoughts, feelings, and motivations, and using this knowledge to portray them on stage or screen. Stanislavsky emphasized the importance of truth and realism in acting, and his approach to training actors, known as the "Stanislavsky Method," focused on developing an actor's ability to connect with their character's emotions and experiences in a genuine way. Through this approach, an actor can create a truly powerful and memorable performance that resonates with the audience.

Chapter 3: The Art of Performance

Bobby Lewis, an American actor and teacher, shared a similar view on the subject of acting. He believed that acting was a process of exploring the truth of human experience and expressing it through the art of performance. For Lewis, the key to successful acting was to cultivate a deep understanding of one's own emotions and experiences, and then use this knowledge to bring a character to life on stage or screen. He emphasized the importance of listening and responding truthfully to one's scene partners, and encouraged actors to use their imagination and intuition to fully inhabit the world of the character. Like Stanislavsky, Lewis believed that acting was a craft that could be taught and refined through rigorous training and practice, and he developed his own approach to actor training, known as the "Lewis Method." Through this method, he sought to help actors discover the truth of their own emotions and experiences, and use this truth to create powerful and authentic performances.

The Lewis Method is not the same as "The Method," developed by Lee Strasberg at The Actors' Studio. Strasberg placed a heavy emphasis on the actors need to work 'from the inside,' relying heavily on their own past emotional experiences and memories of those experiences. Lewis acknowledged the internal work, but was equally at home with actors working first from physical expression of emotions in order to achieve the necessary emotional expression in the moment. He felt that an actor's ability to be truly in the moment while on stage, acting and reacting as if what were happening were real, was more important that the actors' relying on past personal experience.

All of the above is true and interesting, but for me, it fails to touch on a key element of the acting process. That is the moment when an actor feels the character they've been working on 'snap in.' There is a magical moment when you feel you have become that character, and experience the world through their eyes and senses. Of course, you never really lose track of your sense of who you are, but somehow you experience a moment where the character takes over, and thinks and acts, and expresses themselves in ways that you never would. This is the moment, the result, that all of those "methods" I've described, are trying to achieve.

From an interview w/ Meryl Streep:

> *Sybil Thorndike once said, "I think we all have the germ of every other person inside us." And I think we do. I mean I'm not insane. I do know that I'm acting. But you forget about it. Yeah....when you're doing it right, there's a thrilling suspension of the day to day, and you're in somebody else's head.*

One of the things all of these high-sounding definitions fail to mention is that acting involves performing for an audience. That audience might be living human beings, as in the theater, or for cameras if you're acting for television or film. The two experiences (live vs. camera) are very different. Some actors are extremely proficient at both — think Meryl Streep or Hugh Jackman. Others are better suited to one or the other.

Magicians on Acting

This book started its life as a manual for a class I was teaching called "Acting for Magicians." When I was in college, I wanted to be an actor. I took classes in voice production, dialects, movement, mime, stage combat, and many acting classes. Some were great, others seemed like a waste of time to me at the time. I got to be "a pretty decent actor." In New York City, we call those "waiters."

Looking back, I now understand why I couldn't transcend that "pretty good," — competent but not exciting, stage. It had a lot to do with being a young man not quite in touch with my own emotions. As a friend of mine says, "you can't give a gift you don't have," — and I just didn't have that core of strong desires and emotions that audiences would come to the theater or to a film to experience. Or, if I did, I wasn't prepared to express those emotions, even to myself. What I was able to do is pick up a lot of knowledge about how to help others perform better.

Chapter 3: The Art of Performance

Because I had the knowledge and the empathic sense to help others develop their own truly great performances, I went on to get my Masters Degree in Directing for the Theater. I put myself through grad school teaching acting classes!

So, welcome to Acting for Magicians. You're here, so it's unlikely that you question the idea that magicians need to be actors, but just in case, here's what some famous magicians had to say on the subject. Just for fun, I asked Google's AI bot, Gemini, to "Act as a scholar in the Theater Arts Department at an Ivy League institution," and comment on each of the quotes. Here's what I got back (slightly edited):

> *I am delighted to offer a brief commentary on each quotation, highlighting their significance for a magician's growth. Each of these statements underscores the profound kinship between magic and theatrical performance, a relationship that is foundational for any aspiring conjuror.*
>
> *1. "Magic is acting in its purest form." – Doug Henning*
>
> *Commentary:*
> *Henning's assertion distills magic to its theatrical essence. In magic, every gesture, word, and pause must be deliberate—crafted to create belief in the impossible. For the novice, this is a clear challenge: technical skill is only the beginning; the art lies in embodying the illusion so completely that the audience cannot help but be swept away.*
>
> *2. "To be a great magician, you must be an actor playing the role of a magician." – David Copperfield*
>
> *Commentary:*
> *Copperfield reminds us that the magician is a character, not merely a person performing tricks. The "role of a magician" is one of mystery, authority, and charm—qualities that must be convincingly portrayed.*
>
> *Novices should develop a stage persona, understanding that their performance is a narrative, not just a demonstration of skill.*
>
> *3. "A conjuror is an actor playing the part of a magician." – Jean-Eugène Robert-Houdin*

Wired for Wonder

Commentary:
Robert-Houdin, the father of modern magic, emphasizes the performative aspect of conjuring. This quote is foundational: the magician's true craft is in the portrayal, not the mechanics. Notice the similarity to Copperfield's pronouncement, which I suspect was inspired by Robert-Houdin. David is a great student and lover of all things magical.

4. "Magic is a form of theater where the magician is the actor and the magic is the script." – Lance Burton

Commentary:
Burton's analogy positions the magician as both performer and interpreter, with each trick serving as a scene within a script. The magic itself is inert, just the mechanics of illusion, without the performer's interpretation.

Learn to approach each effect as a scene, considering pacing, emotional beats, and dramatic structure.

5. "A magician is an actor, playing the part of a wizard." – Ricky Jay

Commentary:
Jay's statement highlights the fantastical element inherent in magic. The magician's role is to evoke the ancient archetype of the wizard—wise, enigmatic, and powerful.

This inspires beginners to embrace theatricality, enhancing their stage presence by channeling larger-than-life personas.

6. "Magic is an art of illusion, and like acting, it requires the ability to convincingly portray a character." – Penn Jillette

Commentary:
Jillette draws a direct parallel between the illusion of magic and the illusion of character in acting. Both require total commitment to the role. Study character work, ensuring their magical persona is as convincing as any role on stage.

7. "The key to being a great magician is to be a great actor." – Siegfried Fischbacher

Commentary:
Fischbacher's statement is unequivocal: acting is the cornerstone of magical greatness. This is a reminder to develop expressive skills and emotional intelligence alongside technical prowess.

Chapter 3: The Art of Performance

8. *"A magician is essentially an actor who plays the part of someone who can do things that are impossible."* – Derren Brown

Commentary:
Brown articulates the paradox at the heart of magic: the performer must make the impossible seem plausible through sheer conviction. Great magicians must believe in their own performance, as sincerity is infectious and persuasive.

9. *"A magician is a performer, and like all performers, must be able to create an illusion of reality through acting."* – David Blaine

Commentary:
Blaine emphasizes the magician's duty to construct a believable alternate reality, just as any actor in a play must do. Learn the importance of consistency and immersion, ensuring every aspect of their performance supports the illusion.

10. *"Magic is about engaging the imagination of the audience, and like acting, it requires the ability to create a believable character."* – Max Maven

Commentary:
Maven highlights the collaborative nature of magic: it is a shared imaginative act between performer and audience. Remember to focus on audience engagement, cultivating a persona that invites belief and wonder.

11. *"To be a successful magician, you must have the skills of an actor, the knowledge of a scholar, and the heart of a poet."* – Robert E. Neale

Commentary:
Neale's holistic vision elevates magic to a multidisciplinary art. Success requires not just performance, but intellectual curiosity and emotional resonance. This should inspire us to pursue broad education—studying theater, history, literature, and philosophy to enrich our art.

Conclusion

Each quotation, in its own way, insists that magic is not merely the craft of the trickster, but a deeply theatrical art. For the novice magician, embracing these insights means developing not just dexterity and secret techniques, but also empathy, imagination, and presence—the true hallmarks of a master performer. As a performer, you are the instrument - body, voice, emotion - everything. Learning to use that instrument will pay you handsomely!

Introduction to Thinking Like an Actor

Acting is not real life, but it must appear to be real. As a character in a story, there are remarkably fewer distractions than we face in real life. A character is a person with certain desires and goals, who goes after those desires and goals in the face of various obstacles.

Larger stories are made up of many "beats" in which the character with a particular goal is confronted with yet another obstacle. Sometimes the character wins, other times the obstacle wins, and the character must reconsider how they'll reach their ultimate goal. The best stories have lots of these little "reversals." Boring stories just move forward with one win after another for the protagonist.

Each of these little skirmishes is what we call a "beat." It's a small unit of dramatic action. Each time the character fails to win a beat, they change just a bit. The sum of all those changes is what we call the "character arc." String a lot of beats together, and you get a story. Over the course of the story, the character's overall, driving goal becomes apparent, and they are somehow transformed.

Here's an oversimplified example of how a large "want" might break into smaller beats. In this case, the larger goal is, "I really want to take a walk in Central Park." I live on 9th Street, a long way from Central Park, which begins at 59th Street, so there are a lot of small "beats" involved in my achieving the overall goal. First, I have to leave my apartment building. I go to take the elevator, but every time an elevator door opens, the car is already full. I'm frustrated, but I have a way around. I take the stairway and manage to get to the street that way. The first beat of my story is over. I've overcome the conflict of not being able to take the elevator. I win!

Chapter 3: The Art of Performance

Now, I want to get to the subway. It's a two-and-a-half-block walk, and I start off going my "usual" way... but there is a fire in one of the buildings near the end of my block, and the fire department has blocked off the street. I have to go back and around the other direction. As it happens, I run into a friend on the part of the block I don't usually walk on, and we decide to have a cup of coffee together. My trip to Central Park is delayed. Another beat ends, and my story has taken a turn.

I still have that big overall goal, but it looks like we're taking an unintended detour. Will it force me to give up the bigger goal and change my day? Or will I still make it to Central Park? Perhaps there's someone planning to meet me there, someone who will change my life. .. but I don't know they'll be there. Will this chance meeting and coffee with friends prevent that meeting?

Eventually, all of the various beats I encounter will—or will not— get me to my walk in Central Park. Broken down into beats, I might have different small goals, different motivations, every couple of minutes along the way, and will encounter various obstacles to each one. These are my actable moments. That "I want this, now, but that's in the way" is another way of describing the actor's "What's my motivation?" question.

The actor/character must be fully alive and focused within the context of each beat—or we as an audience lose track of the storyline. As a performer, you have the choice at every moment about how strongly you feel about the outcome, and how your body and voice will express that. Bigger choices usually make for a more interesting performance.

Here's another interesting phenomenon: Every actor who performs a role in a play or movie will make different choices, based on their own personalities. As audiences, we are interested in experiencing the character in front of us right now, as performed by this particular performer. If you're performing magic, it's good to remember your audience is there as much to experience you as it is to experience your magic tricks. Are you willing to share your own inner feelings, fears, and joys?

Acting as a Magician

You may well be wondering, "How does all this apply to my new card trick?"

Let's go step by step. Imagine you are seated there at your close-up table, facing a small audience who is there to see some magic. The audience is already getting an impression of you based on what you are wearing, your body language, and the expression on your face.

You stand, and the show has begun. What's in your audience's minds? What are their expectations? As a performer, do you want to meet those expectations, or surprise them... or something else? Let's say you want to meet them.

Your first action beat might be, "Let me put your minds at rest. You're here for miracles, so I'm going to show you a miracle using this deck of cards." And so you take out your deck of cards with that intention. Technically, you just need to get the cards out, but as the character, you're taking them out in order to put their minds at rest and show them something you think they are expecting.

"We magicians do love our decks of playing cards! Let me show you why."

So you're telling them that your purpose is to show what's so special about a deck of cards. Now you've created an expectation, and you need to follow through. This piece needs to end up with a tag that includes, "and that's why magicians love their playing cards so much!"

Now it's time to notice the reactions of your audience. Some are relieved, others disappointed, because they thought they were there for something special... not just some card tricks. You have a choice. Reassure them this won't be your normal, everyday card trick. Or make

Chapter 3: The Art of Performance

them your antagonists. "If you didn't want to see magic, why are you here?"

Whatever your choice—now you're thinking like an artist. It's no longer about, "I need to distract them while I do my double lift," but, "I need to deliver just the right degree of insult in order to get the response I want." Notice that this thinking is always about how you will affect the audience, or the individual person you are speaking to. What will you make them feel? That's your moment-to-moment objective as an actor.

You could have begun another way. "Greetings from the dark side! Who here believes in curses?" Now you're presenting a different character, a different relationship to your audience... and setting different expectations. This time, the story you leave them with is all about the occult and what happens when someone or something is cursed. The playing cards—which you now define as "the devil's playthings"—are your tool for illustrating the curse, but they are no longer the stars of the story.

Our friend Eugene Burger used to say he wanted his magic always to be about more than "the adventures of the props in my hands." That's good advice. Tell better stories, and you'll create better memories.

Every piece of magic can serve one or more purposes. What's your overall goal for this particular piece of magic? Do you want to establish your dominance as a performer? Elicit laughter? Make the audience accept you as one of them? Are you setting up an emotional climate for your next trick? Any one of these can determine your behavior, your scripting, and acting beats for the rest of the trick. If you don't decide, your audience won't know, either.

Audiences want to know you are leading them somewhere, and not just wandering aimlessly. As a performer, your job is to give them a great story and great memories, so decide on what your purpose for each trick is, and then determine your goal for each beat within the story you are acting out.

Shows are actually recursive entities. Each beat, each trick, each piece you present becomes part of something larger—your show. It's important that each one of those has a clear purpose, and that they all work together to create something bigger and more satisfying than just a collection of unrelated tricks.

This holds for all your work as a magician, not just the acting/performance part. As the one writing and creating the script, you need to keep it in mind. The one designing props, costumes, set, and lighting must be on the same path, the same journey. You might fill all those roles yourself, or be working as part of a team. One of my chief jobs as a director is to make sure all the parts serve the overall experience and that there is a clear through line and purpose for that experience.

Your Body is Your Instrument

Your body is your primary visual tool for communicating with your audience. You "embody" a character, and the audience is moved by their response to that embodiment. Of course you also have costumes, props, illusions, and the like—but the body is primary.

When I started working with Jeff McBride, one of the big attractions for me was his use of pantomime, the movement art without speech that causes us to see things that aren't really there. He pounds on an invisible wall, a mask we know isn't really alive or powerful drags him across the stage. Why was Jeff so good at that? Because he had attended the American Mime School in New York, where they trained his mind and body to create those illusions.

Other magicians I've known have studied jazz dance, martial arts, and ballroom dancing in order to make their bodies more expressive and capable.

When I was in college studying acting myself, I took classes in ballet, modern dance, pantomime, fencing, and t'ai chi in addition to

Chapter 3: The Art of Performance

my acting classes. All of those disciplines, and more, can make your body naturally more expressive and interesting for your audiences to watch.

I think it's wise to keep this in mind: When we go to the theater, we're not going to see the same thing we can when watching our neighbor over the fence. We want everything to be a bit "bigger than life." It's your job to deliver that. Bigger movement, bigger sound, bigger emotion. When we're able to make and deliver what I call "bigger choices," we win with our audiences.

At the very least, learn to take care of your body. Learn a good warm-up that will work all your body parts, and do it before every rehearsal and every performance. It makes a bigger difference than you might imagine.

As for magicians who do sleight of hand, we need to take special care to make sure our hands are strong and flexible. Make sure you include your hands in every workout and warm-up.

Which reminds me: Workouts are there to build your body, to make you stronger and more flexible. They will also help keep your body feeling younger and healthier than most of those around you. For magicians, this can include practicing and honing your sleight-of-hand technique.

Warm-ups, on the other hand, are there to make sure you are operating at peak performance levels when you perform. You want to do just enough in a warm-up to make sure all your joints are as flexible as they can be, and your muscles warmed enough to be able to perform at peak. It's very much like tuning a musical instrument just before you go onstage to perform with it.

As an example of a good balance: A dancer on Broadway might spend two or three hours in classes each day, but only 30 to 40 minutes warming up before a show. I know that sounds like a lot, but Broadway dancers are peak performers, doing every night what most others can

Wired for Wonder

only dream of. It's easy to get hurt doing what they do—if you don't warm up properly. And if they don't work in class every day maintaining and improving their technique, they don't last long on Broadway, because Broadway choreographers only hire the best.

A Simple Physical Warm-Up

A good warm-up will make a huge difference in the quality of your performances. Think about it: Musicians wouldn't think of performing in public without first tuning their instruments. Singers do extensive warm-ups before they go onstage. Dancers... well, if they forget to warm up, they're likely to get hurt during performance. So why don't most magicians warm up their instruments, that is, their voices and their bodies?

Here's a basic physical warm-up I've been using for years. It is designed to be easy to remember because we use our body as our mnemonic device, to make sure all of our joints are fully flexible, and that muscles have been warmed up.

Physical Warm-up

The body mnemonic is simple. Start at the top and work down to the bottom.

> *First: Look at the ceiling or sky. Stretch your neck as far as you can to look up. Stretch your face to make it as long as you can while you do this. Then look down. Try and get your chin all the way to your chest as you do this, and scrunch your face to make it as small as you can. Then back up, then down, then up and then down again.*
>
> *Second: Turn your head as far to the right as you can. Really stretch those neck muscles. Then turn it back forward, and then all the way to the left. Go as far as you can so that you really feel the stretch. Do the whole thing again, but let your shoulders go with your head this time. Don't turn your waist. You should be able to look almost directly at the wall behind you, then the one in front of you, then go the other way to look at the wall behind you again. After doing that several times, go ahead and let your waist get*

Chapter 3: The Art of Performance

involved. Now you should be able to go past looking directly behind you! Up to now, we've been moving slow and working to feel the stretch.

Now rotate your head on top of your neck. Try and keep the neck straight up and down as the head does full circles, first one direction and then the other. Then do the whole thing again but let the neck get involved, so that your head is making a very large circle, starting looking down with your chin on the chest, moving to the right, then looking up, then to the left and then back to the chest. Make the circle as large as you can. Do this several times in one direction, then several in the other.

Take a moment to notice how your body, especially the parts we've been moving, feels. It should feel noticeably different than it did before we started.

Third: Now we're going to loosen up just a bit. You'll be letting your arms dangle at your side, and turn your body fairly quickly from one side to the other. Waist, chest, neck, and head all move together, but loosely, and the arms should swing so that your hands flap first against one side, and then the other. We're loosening muscles and joints without exerting much force—just enough to warm them up. You are also loosening up the core of your body, your torso, with this.

At this point, we go back and work on our shoulders just a bit. Most of us hold a lot of tension in our shoulders, and we need to let it go before we can be fully expressive in performance. We start by lifting the shoulders as high as we can, then just dropping them. It's a bit of a tension, then sudden release kind of thing. Up, down, up, down. Then pull your shoulders both as far to the front as you can. Then back to normal, then as far to the back. Do this a couple of times. Finally, we make big circles with both shoulders. All the way to the front, then up, then back, then as far down as we can, and back to the front. Do that three or four times, then reverse directions.

When you're done with the shoulder rolls, shake your whole upper body out, just the way you've seen dogs do, and once again take a moment to notice how your body feels. Include your arms in the shake.

Since we're at arms and hands, and they are especially important for sleight of hand and manipulation magic, let's do some hand warm-ups. First, shake them out. Shake them side to side, then up and down. Make them really floppy and shake as hard as you can without hurting anything. Then make them into fists and squeeze. You should feel the squeeze in your forearms. Do several squeezes, with a release and stretch out flat with fingers fully splayed in between the squeezes.

Now, hold your hands in front of you, and bring your thumbs to your palms, then your forefingers, middle fingers, and so on until you have a tight fist with thumbs inside. Now unfold the fingers, one at a time, making an effort to keep those not yet unfolded fully closed. Do this several times, then repeat, but starting with the little finger instead of the thumb. Now, just wiggle all of your fingers, first keeping them straight, and then making a kind of claw shape and holding them more or less rigid while wiggling them. Finally, repeat the shaking out you did at the beginning.

Take a moment to notice how your hands and arms feel at this point.

This next bit will most likely be difficult the first few times you try it, because it involves isolating your rib cage and its movements, and this is something most of us don't think to do in the course of normal life. The result is that we aren't very coordinated in using and isolating these muscles. After a few days, it becomes quite easy, though.

First, push your chest as far forward as you can. Then contract your chest and push the rib cage backwards as far as you can. Then forward again, back again, and so on. You'll find yourself inhaling when you push forward, and exhaling when going backward if you're doing this right.

Now stop, and—this is the difficult part for most of us—shift the rib cage as far as you can to your right, while keeping your shoulders level. Then bring it back to center and shift it as far as you can to the left. Do it several times, trying to move it further each time.

Now that you've managed to move the rib cage in all four directions, try moving it in a big circle, still keeping your shoulders level. After a few times around the circle, reverse and circle the other direction.

Next come the hips. We'll do essentially the same thing we did with

Chapter 3: The Art of Performance

your rib cage. First, forward as far as you can, then back. Unlike the rib cage, it's fine if the hips tip up and down while you do this. After several times forward and back, move them side to side. Then, make big circles in both directions.

Note that this can be difficult for some men, because we get trained as little boys not to "wiggle our hips." Our anatomy can also make it just a bit difficult. Nonetheless, you can do it, and it's good for you. I find that it helps to imagine I'm standing in a large barrel, and keeping my hips against the rim of the barrel all the way around the circle.

Now that we've loosened the chest and the hips, let's back up just a bit and work on your core. Remember, this is a warm-up, not a substitute for the kind of exercise you would choose to build strength, so we're not doing crunches, sit-ups, or other strength builders. You do want to warm up those core muscles, though, because they're important in real physical expressivity. Martha Graham built her whole modern dance technique on contraction and expansion of these core muscles. So...

You'll want to stand with your arms hanging at your sides, and your weight slightly shifted to the balls of your feet. Take a breath, and then contract your belly muscles with a sharp exhale. Your hands should pull forward. It's exactly the movement you would make if you were punched in the gut, and you might find yourself making the kind of sound you would make if that happened. Hold the contraction for a moment, then take a large breath and let that straighten your body. Go beyond the straight body and actually arch your back a bit as you deepen the breath. Then, sharply, contract again, forcing that sharp exhale. Then expand, contract, expand, contract... and shake out.

Time to take a moment to take stock of how your body feels again. You should be starting to feel energized and more wide awake than you normally do as you go through your days.

At this point, let's work the spine just a bit. Start by standing tall, then dropping your chin to your chest. Then let the weight of your head pull you further over, curling the chest, the belly, and everything else until you're hanging with your arms hanging almost to the ground. If you're a particularly flexible person, your fingers might be touching the ground. The thing about this is to roll down one vertebra at a time, and not to force anything. At this point, if you wish to, you can bend your knees until your fingers do touch the ground, or if you're that flexible person, until the palms of your hands do touch the ground. Leaving them there, you can then stretch your legs out straight. This will really stretch the hamstring muscles and muscles of the lower back. Be careful, though, because you can tweak those lower back muscles. You might want to wait for the leg stretch bit until you've rolled all the way down and all the way back up several times.

After this, it's good to shake your whole body again for a few seconds.

Now the legs. I do squats in fairly slow motion. First place the feet at shoulder width or a bit wider, then bend your legs, lowering your body as far as you can. I studied ballet for several years, so my inclination here is to turn my toes out, but if you've studied martial arts, you might prefer to keep your feet parallel to one another. It's probably best to do this whole section both ways, as that way you'll warm up slightly different combinations of your leg muscles. Do the full squat several times, each time returning to full upright. As you squat, try to keep your torso vertical, almost as though it is riding up and down inside a big tube. If that's too difficult for you at first, it's fine to lean forward as much as you need to.

After three or four repetitions of the squat, I like to end in the full "down" position. I usually spread my feet just a bit further at this point. Now the object is to move your full weight (and position) over one foot, then back to center and then over the other. This stretches the back of your thighs and your groin muscles.

Finally, I stand straight again and shake out. Shake each leg out separately. The shaking is part of what warms up the muscles.

It's time to test your balance. Stand on one leg and flex the other knee and foot. Then extend that leg and point the toes of the foot, slightly out from the body. Flex and stretch it several times.

Then stand on the other leg and do the same.

Finally, stand on the first leg again, lifting the leg slightly to the side, and rotate that foot at the ankle, several times in each direction. Do the same thing on both sides. At this point you've worked almost all of your joints and muscles from the top of your head to the tips of your toes. Good warm-up!

Chapter 3: The Art of Performance

Except you probably haven't even broken a sweat, and breaking a sweat is partly what this is all about. It helps lift your energy in every part of your body, and now that you've loosened things up and gently worked the muscles, it's time to work them all together.

Stand upright with hands hanging loosely at your sides. You should feel relaxed but in a state of readiness. We begin with a deep breath, released slowly with a low growl, as though we're large dogs. Feet keep their toes on the ground, but bounce the heels. It's like running in place, but the object is to use that action to shake all the muscles of your legs. Keep the feet moving, and move the shaking up into your hips, your belly, and your chest. By now your arms should be shaking a bit, so really shake them, the shoulders, and even your head. By now the growl should be loud and a kind of extended shout. Breathe as you might need to. Now get the whole head and face into the shaking and shouting. We end with the hands raised above the head and a huge shout, "Yow!"

This whole process only takes half a minute. It starts slow, but the energy builds as the shaking rises up the body. After a few times doing this, you actually get the sensation that you're drawing energy up from the ground and pumping it up through your body until it shoots out your head. And, if you're really doing it right, and are fully committed, you will break a sweat.

At this point, take a minute or two to take some deep breaths and let your body, heart rate, and breathing return to normal. Except it won't just be "normal"—you'll be fully warmed up and at the energy level you want to be when you begin a performance.

The Voice

One of the primary skills any actor must develop is the use of the human voice. Here are some quotes from great actors you may know, and a commentary, once again from our friend Google Gemini, acting as a senior professor at a prestigious drama school:

Greetings. As a senior faculty member, I've had the privilege of observing how the principles of acting resonate across various performing arts. It's an insightful query to consider these profound quotes from legendary actors and how they might enrich the art of performing magic. Let's delve into each one:

Cicely Berry on the Voice:

Cicely Berry, a renowned voice coach, states, "The voice is an actor's most important tool. It conveys emotion, character, and meaning. You have to know how to use it effectively."

For a performing magician, this is an absolutely critical insight. Far too often, the focus is solely on the mechanics of the illusion, but the presentation is what truly creates magic. Your voice isn't just for delivering patter; it's a powerful instrument for directing attention, building suspense, expressing your character (whether mysterious, comedic, or intellectual), and conveying the "magic" itself. Consider how a subtle change in vocal tone can make a simple "watch closely" either ominous or playful, or how your pacing can dictate the rhythm of the audience's attention. Mastering vocal techniques—projection, articulation, modulation, and emotional resonance—allows a magician to truly command the stage and deepen the audience's experience of wonder.

Alan Rickman on Craft, Discipline, and Training:

Alan Rickman, an actor celebrated for his meticulous approach, observed, "Acting is a craft, and like any craft, it requires discipline and training. Physical and vocal training are essential to develop the skills necessary to bring a character to life."

This quote directly addresses the often-overlooked aspect of performance in magic. While magicians dedicate countless hours to perfecting sleight of hand or prop manipulation, Rickman reminds us that the act of performing itself is a distinct craft requiring its own rigorous discipline. For magicians, this means going beyond just knowing the trick. It involves dedicated physical training to refine stage presence, gestures, misdirection through subtle body language, and graceful movement. Simultaneously, vocal training is essential for clear, engaging communication, emotional expressiveness, and building a compelling rapport with the audience. This holistic training develops the essential skills needed to transform a mere trick into a truly captivating and lifelike magical experience.

Sanford Meisner on Truthful Behavior and Control:

Sanford Meisner, whose acting technique emphasizes authentic behavior, said, "Acting is behaving truthfully under imaginary

Chapter 3: The Art of Performance

circumstances. To do that, you have to have a strong foundation of physical and vocal control."

This is perhaps the most profound point for a magician. Every magical performance is, at its heart, the creation of an "imaginary circumstance"—a moment where the impossible becomes real. To make this illusion believable, the magician must "behave truthfully" within that imaginary world. This means that your reactions to the "magic"—whether it's surprise at an outcome, calm confidence in your abilities, or feigned difficulty with a prop—must appear genuine to the audience. This genuine appearance is underpinned by strong physical control (e.g., the precise timing of a gesture, the holding of a gaze to direct attention, or maintaining composure during a reveal) and impeccable vocal control (e.g., delivering your script with convincing emotion, reacting authentically to audience gasps, or maintaining a consistent character voice). It is through this mastery of control that the magician can effectively sell the illusion and make the audience truly believe in the magic unfolding before their eyes.

In essence, these quotes underscore that magic, like all forms of acting, is not just about technique; it's about authentic storytelling, compelling presence, and masterful communication, all built upon a foundation of dedicated physical and vocal training.

Vocal Warm-up

When I'm going to perform, I generally follow the physical warm-up I described above with this vocal warm-up. It's useful to have your body fully functional before working with the voice, because it's actually all connected.

We begin by taking a few slow deep breaths, and letting each go with a sigh. After two or three of those, you begin to let your vocal cords come together enough to make the sound audible. Don't close them down yet to make a hard sound, but just let the sigh and soft vocalization warm them up. Relax your jaw and face as much as you can, and make sure you're breathing all the way down from your diaphragm. If you place your hand on your belly, just below the ribs, you'll feel the diaphragm working. Just relax, breathe, and sigh for several minutes.

Wired for Wonder

It helps to have knowledge of how the voice works, so here is a simple, layman's description.

There are four main components of the human voice. First is the breath. Learn to breathe deeply by habit, because the more breath you have to work with, and the better you control it, the better control you'll have of all the other elements. So start by taking several deep, deep breaths, from the diaphram.

The second part of vocal production is the vocal cords themselves. These are two flaps of muscle at the side of your larynx. They aren't really cords in the sense of big strings, but more like flaps. In any event, when you bring the edges together and blow air across them, they produce sound. Do that now, allowing a kind of sighing sound to escape. At this point, we've been blowing air through, but not tightening the cords enough to produce the usual "hard" sound we use most of the time when speaking or singing.

Now go ahead and make that harder sound. Take a deep breath and let it out with an "ah" sound. Whatever pitch is most natural is the right one. It should feel as though you are singing the tone, keeping your jaw relaxed and letting the breath out fully, so that the sound lasts five or ten seconds. Pay attention to the feel of the vocal cords coming together, and listen to the sound as it comes out.

Note: As we get used to taking deeper breaths, sometimes we want to fill the upper chest with air as well as the lower parts. Instead, breathe almost exclusively from your diaphragm. If you breathe using the rib cage and muscles around it, you'll wind up straining your vocal cords, because the muscles that control them are also part of the system that controls breathing in the upper rib cage. Of course, if you want to produce more distorted sounds, this is a way to do that. However, you will eventually grow hoarse, or actually damage the vocal cords if you do too much of that.

After several repeats, see if you can refine your control of the breath and the vocal cords in order to prolong the amount of time you can sing that "ah." Don't strain. This isn't about forcing anything, only learning better control.

Next, close your lips, and hum the same tone. We're moving on to the third main element of vocal production, which is resonance. Where your voice resonates determines a great deal of how it will sound.

Chapter 3: The Art of Performance

Have you ever stretched a rubber band and plucked it? It makes a tinny little twang. Hold the same rubber band across the mouth of a cup or a bowl, and pluck it, and you'll hear an entirely different sound. It's the same with the sounds your vocal cords produce.

So, hum, and explore making different parts of your face and throat vibrate as you hum. You can make your lips vibrate, your nose, your forehead, the throat itself. Try making chewing motions as you hum, as though you've taken a big bite of something and it barely fits in your mouth. Chew the sound as you hum, and explore what it feels like to make it resonate in different places. When you've practiced for a while, you can even make your chest and belly vibrate with your sound.

Through all of this, be careful not to push the volume too much. You can play with getting louder and softer, but don't overdo. Remember, we're just warming up the different vocal components.

After you've explored all the ways you can make your face and body vibrate using the humming, let's open our mouths. Hold your hand out, flat, as though you're about to pat your open mouth, and see if you can make an "ah" sound that makes the palm of your hand vibrate. Move it further away and closer, experimenting with the different ways you can make the voice resonate and bounce the sounds off your hand. Make sure your jaw is still relaxed, and that you're producing the sound right on the edge of the cords.

Before ending this portion of our warm-up, let's make ourselves aware of how speaking different vowel sounds affects our resonance. We'll use the sound "aum," or, more accurately, "A (as in 'at'), ah, aw, o, ou, oo, eeeee" all run together. Take a big breath and open your mouth loosely. Make the "a" sound, and notice that it resonates at the bottom and front of the mouth. The tongue is flat and the sound on the tip of the tongue. Continue to the "ah" portion of the sound, and feel the resonance slide back to the middle of the tongue, still low in the mouth. As you slide toward the big "o" sound, the resonance moves to the back of the throat, then up toward the hard palate as you round your lips and move to the "oo" sound. Keep moving toward the "eee" sound, now resonating at the top of the mouth and down to come out between the teeth. Do this whole thing several times, exploring how your tongue, cheeks, and lips move as you do it.

Now it's time to begin working on the fourth element of vocal production, articulation. We use the tongue, lips, teeth, and cheeks to articulate. There is a wonderful scene from one of my favorite movies, Singin' in the Rain, where Gene Kelly and Donald O'Connor spoof a voice lesson. "Moses supposes his toeses are roses..." This pretty much sums up the kind of exercises we do to warm up and improve our articulation or diction. The idea is to use repetitive tongue twisters to exercise your mouth around every possible consonant sound, and tongue twisters do this. They don't have to be difficult, but tend to be more fun when they are.

(Note: In my last book, *The Performer's Edge*, I teach a version of "The Announcers' Test" which is a fun and fairly complete warm-up for all of the consonants. Find it on YouTube)

For an easy warm-up, I usually begin with some of the following, repeated again and again, over-enunciating each sound. If you over-enunciate when warming up, your mouth will enunciate naturally but more clearly when you're actually performing. Here we go:

- Typical, topical, typical, topical. Topeka, Topeka, Topeka, Topeka

- Miminy, mominy, miminy, mominy

- Ta da sa, ta da za, ta da sa, ta da za

- Seven silly sisters sat sewing in the sand

- Around the rugged rock the ragged rascal ran

- Red leather, yellow leather, red leather, yellow leather

- She sells seashells down by the seashore

- Betty Botter bought some butter, but she said this butter's bitter

- Unique New York, Unique New York

If you have difficulty with any particular sound (I did with sibilant "s" sounds... which I corrected with the "ta da sa, ta da za" exercise above, done for five minutes every day for a month), you can find a particular phrase to help you conquer that difficulty asking Google. "I have difficulty pronouncing the sound -----. Is there a tongue twister

Chapter 3: The Art of Performance

designed to help me correct this?"

Okay... your vocal production system is now at least somewhat warmed up. There are many other things you can do in order to enhance your speaking voice, though. One is just singing. Do you sing in the shower? It's fun, and if you're not bothering anyone, a great way to start building vocal power.

Another way is to take the scripts for the pieces you perform, and sing them. Turn them into opera, or pop music, or whatever your favorite kind of music is. I'm rather fond of the exaggerations of opera, because singing your script that way helps you become aware of emotional highs and lows you might not discover if you just speak the script.

Another useful vocal training technique is to go into a large space like a theater or a gym, and speak to an imaginary person, first just a few feet from you, as though you're performing across the dinner table, then a few yards further away, then a few more and a few more until you're speaking to the (imaginary) person who is as far away as they could possibly be within that space. Don't shout. Just focus your voice on that person and make sure they can hear you. If you have a friend willing to do this with you, that's helpful. The idea is to focus your voice without straining or shouting. I can't really describe the details of how this works, but once you've tried it a few times, you will figure it out for yourself.

Rehearsal

I know many magicians who will put in hours practicing a new sleight or handling of a prop—but they don't believe they need to rehearse. Some don't even like to write a script, because they feel it will hamper their spontaneity. What not scripting and rehearsing really does is hamper your career.

Our friend Mac King will tell you, "I don't really have a script." He means he hasn't written his script down. Mac came up doing comedy clubs, two shows a night. As a comic magician, he would try different things every night—until they clicked in. Then they didn't change. If you see Mac's show two, three, or more times (you should!), you'll notice that the words are 99% exactly the same from show to show. So is his blocking, his prop handling—virtually everything except for what his various volunteers do. Even when a volunteer does something "unexpected," Mac is ready with a line he has prepared, and knows will get the right reaction. After hundreds of nights in those comedy clubs, Mac was very well rehearsed. After thousands of shows in Las Vegas, his show runs like a well-oiled machine. So, although he "doesn't have a script, and doesn't really need to rehearse," in actuality he is very well scripted and has the amazing polish and confidence that only comes with being well-rehearsed.

Notice that I said you have to go back to Mac's show several times before you'll realize how tightly scripted it really is. That's because all that rehearsal and repetition has engraved the show into Mac's brain to the point where he now just works on making it seem real and off-the-cuff. He's acting, and doing it so well that you won't catch him until you've seen the show more than once.

What's the difference, you may well ask, between practicing your magic and rehearsing? Practicing is the act of repeating a skill over and over until it is burned into your neurons, and you no longer have to think about it. Rehearsal, on the other hand, is the act of repeating your complete performance of a piece of magic over and over, as though an audience is there watching, until you no longer have to think about the words, the movement—or anything except your interaction with your audience.

You get to cross into that magical space where you become the character you are pretending to be. They come to life, and your performance feels real, both to you and your audience.

One of Eugene Burger's favorite aphorisms was that "Thinking kills magic." Why? Because if you have to think about your technique, the words you'll use, or anything other than your interaction with your

Chapter 3: The Art of Performance

audience—and remember, in magic, the audience is your acting partner in the performance—you'll fail to be "real" in the moment. The audience will be reminded that what they are experiencing is a fake, and the magic you want them to feel will evaporate.

Here's a paradox: All of the best "improvisers" are extremely well rehearsed. This comes from the traveling comedy troupes that existed from the time of the Greeks onward. The best known were the Italian commedia dell'arte troupes, made up of a dozen or so characters, each of whom played a stock character. Each character had dozens of stock bits and speeches they had rehearsed and rehearsed—things like a funny bit catching an imaginary fly, or a stock speech to be delivered to a lover. The bits and speeches could be mixed and matched to fit many different kinds of stories, so performances would appear to be completely spontaneous and improvised. To some extent they were—but all the best bits had been rehearsed again and again, until they seemed to arise completely in the moment, out of the action.

Part of the fun in this is that, when you have tried-and-true, fully rehearsed bits that you know will carry your performance, you then become free to improvise with whatever happens in the moment, because you know you'll be coming back to that killer ending of a piece, the thing that always works.

Rehearsal for Discovery

Once you've chosen a piece of magic, and have at least a rough idea of a story it will tell, it's time to play! In the theater, early rehearsals are the time for actors to explore. We try different blocking, different bits of business, different ways of interpreting our lines. We explore different kinds of connections between our characters. This is where the form the performance will ultimately take all comes together.

As a magician, this is the time to try different ways of presenting. Do you make your moves bigger and broader, or smaller and more subtle? You can explore different motivations for different moves you must make. There are things that are required for you to execute the particular piece of magic, and other things you do as part of telling your story to the audience. This is the time when you can experiment with different ways of making the technical moves seem like they are moves from the story.

For example, there are many times in magic where you pretend to place an object from one hand to the other. You know you have to do it, or pretend to do it, in order to make the magic work. But your audience needs to have a reason that your character does that. Maybe it's showing the object to one side of the audience, and then the other. Maybe it's that something seems out of place and you need to use the hand holding the object to fix things, so you move it to the other hand. There can be multiple possible reasons for each move—and this part of the rehearsal period is when you are figuring that out by trying different things.

It's also the time when you can discover ways to make your character bigger and more interesting. You can practice increasing your vocal range by singing, shouting, or whispering the lines. You can perform the whole piece without saying the lines, but making sure every bit of the piece is understandable through pantomime. You can perform the whole three-minute piece in 30 seconds... or in slow motion so that it will take you 10 minutes to get through it. Each of these arbitrary explorations will teach you different things you can do to make the piece better.

Rehearsal for Polish

At some point, you have to "set" your piece. This means that you've decided on every move, every line, every inflection. Now it's time to run the piece another 20 or 30 times as though you are in front of an audience. No stopping and starting over if something goes wrong. If it does go wrong, cover exactly as you will if and when it happens in front of a paying audience.

This is when you are burning the piece into your nervous system. The object is to get it to the place where you no longer need to think

Chapter 3: The Art of Performance

about the moves, the words, or any of the other technical matters involved. You're getting ready to try the piece out for an audience, and when that happens, you want your attention to be completely on interacting with that audience.

There is another stage for every show, every piece of magic or theater. On Broadway, we rehearse a show in its "discovery" phase for the first week or week and a half. Then we polish for another week and a half, right up through technical rehearsals, when we are performing with full sound and lights, and dress rehearsal, where it all has to be nearly perfect.

But after that three weeks of various kinds of rehearsal, we have previews. This is a time when audiences first see the show, and respond to it. The audience response always changes the show. Typically, a show will have a preview in the evening, then a rehearsal the next afternoon to change things that didn't work.

I remember when I got to work on the first production of *Sweeney Todd* on Broadway. We got to the first preview, and the show was a mess. Razors designed to squirt fake blood across the stage squirted it all over most of the audience. An elevator bridge designed to move, with actors on it, failed to work properly. There were segments of the story that just didn't make sense to the audience, and they hated the show.

Actors' Equity has a special provision for this kind of situation. They allow actors to rehearse for a week or so "ten out of twelve" hours during previews, because they recognize the urgency of making a show work, and the fact that everyone involved has invested so much already.

For *Sweeney Todd*, the process was a success. The difference between the first preview and opening night was amazing to see, and the show went on to win nine Tony Awards.

With magic, this time is even more crucial. Our audiences don't just sit back in their chairs and enjoy what they see. They participate, and we really don't know how they'll respond until we've had a number of them do that. So we need to find ways to make sure they do respond as we want them to... and we can't really know that until we have our show in front of them. For the first 20 or 30 performances of a new piece, you'll find you have to go through the whole rehearsal process—discover, polish, and preview—after each performance.

This, by the way, is the crucial difference between the polished "master" magician like Jeff McBride and the talented upstart. While the upstart may shine one night, they'll fall on their face the next. The master will be consistent, and their worst night will be better than that talented upstart.

One last thing before I leave the subject of rehearsal. We live in a time where it costs you virtually nothing to record every rehearsal and performance. Get a tripod and set up your smartphone or other camera to cover the whole stage or rehearsal space. Have an usher turn it on before the show begins... and watch it when you get home! You'll find ways—after practically every show—that you can improve. Ways you want to change posture, inflection of a particular line, put in or take out a pause, remember to make eye contact—there's always something. The performer who fixes just one thing after every performance will have a huge advantage over the ones who don't. So... how good do you want to be?

How Venues Shape Performance

Imagine for a moment that you are speaking with your best friend, over a table at your local café. You're only a foot or two apart, and the noise of the café masks your conversation from those around you. You feel their presence, and they, yours. You are free to discuss intimate personal matters if you wish, or your latest embarrassing escapade on the dating scene. You naturally know how to speak so your friend hears you, but not the whole café.

Chapter 3: The Art of Performance

Now imagine trying to have that same conversation inside a large gym—perhaps from opposite ends of a basketball court. The gym is filled with fans, all making noise, so you have to shout if you want to be heard. You might have to wave your arms, jump up and down, or engage in some kind of giant, elaborate pantomime, just to make yourself understood to your friend at the other end of the court. And discussing anything "private" is completely out of the question, because there are several thousand "fans" hanging on your every utterance.

Let's imagine a third situation—larger than that one-on-one and smaller than the stadium. Now we're in a church. Light filters through stained-glass windows. A choir sings somewhere in the building, the sound filling the space. There's incense in the air.

In each of these situations, we experience things differently. We communicate differently, and our relationships with the other people in the space are different. We might say exactly the same words in each situation, but the experience will be different. And when we perform magic—or any kind of theater, for that matter—in any of those different spaces, it has to be a different kind of magic.

Each space carries its own expectations, each is built for different purposes. In one, we whisper. Another requires shouting. In one, the subtlest movement, the slightest shift in emotion, is effective. One is built for crowd reactions, another for intimate conversation, and the third for reverence.

What Each Space Demands

Magic in the café relies on proximity and subtlety. Your sleight of hand happens inches from spectators' eyes. You can speak quietly, tell stories that unfold slowly, create moment s of genuine astonishment because you're controlling exactly what each person sees and when. That slightly risqué story driving your funniest close-up piece works perfectly here—you're having a conversation, not giving a speech.

Wired for Wonder

The gym demands the opposite. Everything must read from a distance. Your magic needs to be big, visual, instantly comprehensible. Subtle shifts in facial expression vanish at 50 feet. A whispered aside is impossible. But scale and spectacle become available to you—productions, appearances, transformations that would overwhelm an intimate setting. The audience becomes a collective entity responding as one, creating energy that feeds back to you onstage.

The church represents something between those extremes, but with its own unique character. There's space, but also focus. The architecture directs attention. The atmosphere suggests something more than entertainment—perhaps wonder, perhaps mystery. Comedy might work here, but irreverence probably won't. The audience expects something that respects the setting's inherent dignity.

The Mistake of Bringing the Wrong Magic

I've known more than one magician, hired for the first time to do strolling magic at a corporate party, who brought only intimate, script-driven pieces that required quiet conversation with spectators. This often works beautifully at parties—it's café magic in a social setting. But when the band starts playing or the crowd gets loud, suddenly you're trying to perform gym magic without the right material. You need quick, visual hits that grab attention and entertain for a few moments, then release the spectators back to their party. No long buildups. No patter that requires them to hear every word.

The magician who succeeds in that environment carries both types of material and reads the room.

Sometimes Conventional Wisdom Is Wrong

Years ago, I booked Jeff McBride to tour with the 50th anniversary show of the Radio City Rockettes. The show's manager was concerned about Jeff's "Sorcerer's Apprentice" version of The Miser's Dream—a piece where coins appear repeatedly at the magician's fingertips. The manager worried that in those giant theaters, people in the back rows wouldn't be able to see the coins. It seemed like a valid concern.

Chapter 3: The Art of Performance

But it was based on a false premise—that seeing the coins was what the piece was about.

The way Jeff performs this piece, it's actually about his wordless interaction with a young boy selected from the audience and brought onstage. The boy goes through a kind of initiation, becoming a magician himself. Coins appear and go immediately into a large bucket, making a loud noise easily heard throughout the theater. Jeff reacts. The boy reacts. And the audience reacts to their reactions. Night after night, the piece stopped the show.

The lesson? Don't mistake the surface mechanics of a piece for its actual engine. Jeff had adapted his magic by finding elements that worked at scale—sound, relationship, emotional dynamics—rather than assuming everything depended on visual detail alone.

Reading Your Venue

Before you perform anywhere new, visit the space if you possibly can. Walk the room and ask yourself these questions:

Scale and distance: How far is the back row? Can you make eye contact with individuals, or will you primarily see the audience as a mass? Does the space feel intimate even if it's large, or does it create distance even when it's small?

Acoustics: Can you speak conversationally and be heard? Will you need to project? Is there ambient noise—music, HVAC, traffic—that will compete with you? Can you use sound as an element, like Jeff's coin bucket?

Atmosphere and expectations: What happens in this space normally? Is it a place of reverence, celebration, or transaction? Does the architecture create formality or intimacy? What kind of experience will the audience expect just by virtue of being in this room?

Technical realities: Where will you enter and exit? If you use tables or rolling equipment, can they move easily? Will the audience look up at you or down at you? What's the lighting like?

These questions map back to our three archetypes. You're diagnosing whether you're in the café, the gym, or the church—and choosing or adapting your material accordingly.

The slightly risqué story that kills in the café might need to be cut for the church. The subtle color change that amazes at close range needs to become a bigger transformation for the gym. The comedy piece that plays as irreverent fun in one space might come across as disrespectful in another.

We might say exactly the same words in different venues, but the experience will be different. Smart performers know this and prepare accordingly. They don't just bring their best material—they bring the right material for the space they're in.

Chapter 4

Show Tech

There are always technical considerations, no matter what kind of show you are performing. From the way the street performer designs and transports their set-up on up to performances in giant theaters with extensive sound, lighting and video support. As magicians, we're probably more concerned with our personal tech— our props, costumes, etc., than most other performers.

Let's examine each of the main technical areas, and how it will affect your performances.

The Space

We've established that performance space—and the resulting relationship to your audience—makes a huge difference. That intimate card trick you perform tableside won't play at Radio City Music Hall. Conversely, Siegfried & Roy's grand illusions ultimately needed a massive, custom showroom to reach their full potential. Both situations can provide transformative experiences, but only when you understand their strengths and limitations.

Every venue presents unique challenges: stage size, audience distance, sightlines. As a magician, certain tricks shift from magical to instructional depending on viewing angle. Arrive early to every theater and check every angle that matters. Don't just scan side to side—climb to the balcony and check from above. Sit front row, looking up at the stage. Can those spectators see into your table? Spot the water in bowls that should appear empty? Notice the gimmick hanging behind that silk?

Learn everything possible about your venue before arrival, and always build in enough time to adjust your show if needed.

Wired for Wonder

When I arrived at Ford's Theatre in Washington—where Lincoln was assassinated—Jeff McBride was performing in a presidential variety show. Jeff used a wheeled table for quick transitions, but I'd forgotten Ford's stage was raked, slanting downward toward the audience. This Victorian-era design improved sightlines and acoustics for declamatory performances, but it created a problem: Jeff's table would've rolled straight into the President's lap.

Fortunately, the Ford's stagehands had encountered this before. They produced a small wedge-shaped platform that leveled just enough space to secure the table. We solved this during dress rehearsal the day before. Had we arrived mere hours before showtime, we would've been in serious trouble.

A ventriloquist colleague once performed for a youth organization at their venue. Despite her detailed tech rider, they'd arranged all the sound and lighting equipment perfectly—but hadn't considered power. The nearest outlets were over 200 feet from the stage, and no one had plugged anything in to test it.

She'd arrived six hours early, giving her time to dispatch someone to buy several hundred feet of heavy-duty extension cord. Crisis averted.

The lesson bears repeating: Always arrive early. Research your venue thoroughly beforehand and prepare for every contingency. Murphy's Law guarantees that eventually, something will go wrong. But with proper preparation, you'll handle it before curtain.

Light

Many strolling and street performers tell me, "I don't have to think about lighting because I never control it." While you can't request specific lighting in these situations, you still have agency.

Nearly every venue has lighter and darker areas—spaces with ambient light versus directional, shadow-casting light. Arrive well before your performance and ask them to set lights as they'll be during

Chapter 4: Show Tech

the event. Scout the room. Find where lighting works best for your performance. Some strolling magicians carry small flashlights to distribute among spectators, improving visibility while drawing attention to the performance.

The Power of Lighting

Light directs attention and sets emotional tone more powerfully than most performers realize. In traditional theater spaces, we have access to numerous tools that shape audience experience. Why not use them well?

Here are some fundamental lighting principles:

Brightness commands attention. The brightest object onstage draws the eye. Want audiences watching you? Be the brightest thing in their field of vision. Want them focused on that grand illusion rolling onstage? Light that instead.

Placement matters. Traditional theater and film lighting creates "natural" effects. Natural light comes from sources—sunlight, fire, lamps—usually positioned above us. Lighting designers typically place the main "key" light about 45 degrees above and 45 degrees to one side of the performer.

Key light alone creates drama, not naturalism. In reality, light bounces off surroundings and fills spaces with softer illumination. Add diffuse "fill" light from the opposite 45/45 angle, and your lighting reads as natural.

Unconventional placement signals unusual situations. Remember holding a flashlight under your chin to look like a monster? That's extreme low-angle lighting. Move your key light from the standard position, and suddenly you're on a moonlit street, in a dungeon, or on a vaudeville stage with footlights.

Back lighting creates depth. Positioned behind the performer—anywhere from floor level to high above—back lighting produces glowing silhouettes. Combined with front light, it creates a halo that

Wired for Wonder

separates you from the background. For magicians who wear dark clothing against dark backdrops, back lighting prevents you from disappearing.

Side lighting emphasizes movement. Lights positioned at waist level from stage sides enhance full-body movement and dance. Professional dance concerts feature entire banks of side lights for this purpose.

Powerful as these alternative positions might be, as a magician you must use back and side lighting carefully. That back light will reveal the object hidden behind your silk before you want it seen. Lights from the side might call attention to places where you've hidden objects you intend to produce as though from nowhere.

Experimenting with Light

Find a room with a full-length mirror, grab a flashlight, and kill the lights. Watch yourself in the mirror as you move the flashlight around. Hold it beneath your chin—there's your monster. Move it overhead and notice how dramatically your face changes as you shift it forward, directly above, then behind you. Try side lighting. You become different characters depending on how light defines you. Add a second flashlight and explore how positioning each light transforms your appearance.

Color and Focus

Color creates emotion. Soft blue-green moonlight affects audiences differently than bright white sunlight. In a theater, we can shift stage color instantly or gradually, guiding emotional response.

What you choose to illuminate matters, too. Lighting the entire stage sends one message. A tight spotlight on only the performer sends another entirely. We feel diffrently about several objects and people on the stage if each is in a small pool of light than we do if the whole stage is brightly lit around them.

Chapter 4: Show Tech

House Lights and Audience Connection

Theater convention dictates that house lights drop before stage lights rise, signaling the transition into "story space"—a dreamlike state where audience interaction differs from real life. For magicians, this creates a tension. We want interaction. We want to cross the fourth wall. We don't want our audience sitting in darkness.

My solution: Begin in complete darkness, capitalizing on those powerful moments. But by the end of the opening performance piece, house lights have gradually risen to half brightness. The audience still senses they're in a special space, set apart from the stage space, but the magician can see and interact with them. For participatory moments, I often bring house lights to full, then return to half when the interaction ends.

Great lighting design works almost subliminally. After the show, audiences sense that something changed throughout—but if you've done it well, their attention stayed on the action, only peripherally on the lighting. That peripheral effect profoundly shapes their emotional response.

Special Considerations for Magic

Working with threads under bright lighting is challenging. While possible to light thread-suspended objects without revealing the thread, it's difficult. The best solution: a bright, busy, detailed backdrop. Metallic ribbon or sparkly curtains work well. The thread is actually visible, but the audience just sees the noise around it. Most effective: LED screen imagery. Marco Tempest once flew small lights on 50-pound fishing line inside a stadium against giant LED backdrops. The lines remained invisible, as long as the LED screen was lit.

Remember: back and side lighting, though visually striking, can expose secrets—that object behind the silk or the large screen your assistants just carried on becomes visible before you want it to.

Naturalism vs. Spectacle

There's a time for naturalistic lighting that focuses attention entirely on the performer and their actions. There's another time for rock concert lighting—sweeping beams, strobes, and effects. Rock concert lighting adds excitement but calls attention to itself, signaling that what we're seeing isn't quite real. Both approaches have legitimate uses.

Learning More

Today's lighting designers have extensive options for instruments and control systems. If you work in theaters, corporate events, or casinos, invest time learning this art. Start with *The Stage Lighting Handbook* by Frances Reid or *Designing with Light: An Introduction to Stage Lighting* by J. Michael Gillette and Michael McNamara. Both are comprehensive college texts covering contemporary stage lighting.

Sound

Like all theatrical elements, sound plays a crucial role in performance. You've likely discovered that sound enhances illusion—the click pass, a clown's squeaker, and your spoken script all rely on audio.

When I was learning to act, most actors didn't use amplification, even on Broadway. Voice projection was fundamental training—learning to be understood from the back row without shouting or straining. It's possible, but increasingly rare, because the landscape has shifted.

Today we use amplification in almost every performance situation. Microphones—handheld, lavalier, headset, or stand-mounted—are standard equipment. Add amplifiers, speakers, mixers, and music sources, and suddenly you need to be technologically literate even to work as a self-contained performer.

Using Microphones

Each microphone type requires different skills. Handheld mics come in two basic varieties: unidirectional and omnidirectional.

Chapter 4: Show Tech

Unidirectional mics only capture sound in line with themselves. Speak off-axis and they won't pick it up. Omnidirectional mics pick up sound from all directions. Each has its advantages.

Jeff McBride prefers unidirectional handhelds because they give him complete sound control. Point the mic away from a volunteer, and the audience doesn't hear them. Drop it to his side, and he can give instructions to a volunteer that the audience won't catch. This directional control proves invaluable in ways other mic types can't match. It also keeps control in his hands rather than relying on a sound operator—essential for one-off corporate events where there's insufficient rehearsal time to coordinate subtle cues like a three-second mic cut. It also requires that he choreograph his movements holding the mic, or placing it on or off its stand.

Many other performers prefer headset mics. These connect to a belt-clipped transmitter/battery pack, leaving your hands free while providing security—you always know where the mic is. You can control on/off from the transmitter, but will probably rely on your sound technician to turn it on and off as needed. If you buy your own system, verify that your equipment interfaces with venue sound systems. Always contact their sound tech a few days ahead to confirm you have proper connection cables.

The Battery Question

On Broadway, I watched sound techs replace batteries in all 35 actor mics before every performance. Surely the batteries didn't die that quickly?

"No, but they deteriorate at different rates. I need precise control for each mic. If the signal varies even slightly day to day, it affects sound balance." For a major Broaday musical, this matters.

Music and Cues

Jeff calls many of his music cues directly from stage, eliminating the operator's need to guess timing. He uses a casual, friendly approach:

109

Wired for Wonder

"Hey, Bob! Could we have the Moonlight Music here?" This draws attention to the mechanics, but when there's no stage manager calling cues, it ensures precise timing.

Using music to underscore magic is a professional secret super power. Like good lighting, music tells your audience what to feel—soft, mournful, energetic, building excitement. Watch any film scene with sound off, then with sound on. The difference is staggering. It can be the same for your magic, if you take the time to use it well.

Murphy's Law

That said, if something technological is going fail during performance, it's usually sound equipment. Cables break. Batteries die. Wireless frequencies get overrun by other equipment. Sound technicians get distracted.

"Mastery is when everything that can go wrong has gone wrong, and you've learned how to deal with it."

Chapter 5
The Team

Theater is a collaborative art. Even if you see yourself as a one-person operation, there are many jobs to be done in order to make a theatrical experience come together. Here's a description of some of those jobs, as done in traditional theater. You might be working in a different situation, but learning these roles and why they are needed will help you take care of their functions in almost any situation you might find yourself.

Director

The director's job is multifaceted. First, they help you create vision and structure for your show. What will it be about? How will you provide exciting flow that keeps audiences engaged and delivers a sense of completion? The director serves as CEO of the show, pulling together all elements—sound, lights, staging, costumes, choreography. They are there to help you improve and elevate your performance.

The director attends every rehearsal, giving notes to you and your team. She helps stage the show for smooth flow with seamless transitions and clear beginning, middle, and end.

A director's primary job is ensuring all show elements work together to focus audience attention where it needs to be for the best possible experience. She provides that essential "third eye" that sees everything and makes adjustments toward a common goal. This perspective is nearly impossible when you're standing onstage as one of those elements.

Working with Theater-Trained Directors

Most theater directors have been trained to work differently than we do in magic. They're accustomed to receiving a finished script, holding auditions to cast the perfect ensemble, and arriving at rehearsals with their vision largely set. The director has the final word on every aspect of a production.

In magic, you've likely already created most of the material for your show. You'll collaborate with your director to fulfill the role normally filled by the playwright.

Additionally, theatrical directors work with actors, singers, and dancers trained in methods the director understands and takes for granted. Your director likely won't fully grasp the intricacies required to make a trick work. They'll suggest things like, "Turn right here and come three steps closer to the audience," not realizing that turning that way reveals the load hanging at your back, and moving closer exposes the method to half the house.

Theater directors are also accustomed to productions that maintain a strict "fourth wall," with action contained entirely onstage between actors. The usual audience role is simply to laugh and applaud when inspired. They will not have dealt with our common process of bringing audience members onstage, and all the considerations surrounding that phenomenon.

Because of these differences, magicians sometimes struggle working with directors. That's unfortunate, because directors can learn what they need to work effectively with magicians, and a good director can vastly improve your show — more quickly and effectively than you probably imagine — once you learn to collaborate.

What Working with a Director Looks Like

Imagine working on a Miser's Dream routine. The director asks you to set up—table, props, costume whatever will be a part of the piece.

Chapter 5: The Team

"Let me see you run it once."

You perform. Introduce the piece, produce the first coin, drop it in the bucket, continue through to the end.

"OK, let's start with the introduction. You tell us the history of 'The Miser's Dream,' who originated it, how other magicians performed it, and that this is your unique version. I felt like I was in a lecture about magicians, not at a show. Do you really need all that? Can we create an introduction more about what the piece will be? What do you see as the purpose, the theme of this piece?"

That's called "giving a note." It can sting, because we resist letting go of elements we've worked hard to create. Save time by responding, "OK. How should we change it?" The wrong response: "Well, it has to be that way because..." Arguments with your director usually just protect your ego and aren't productive. She's not attacking you—she's helping make your piece more effective. She won't always be right, but try her suggestions. If she's wrong, you'll both know quickly and move on.

Typical notes address timing and rhythm. You might need more pauses, or to slow down or speed up specific sections. Are you looking up and checking in with your audience at applause moments, or running over them? The director helps by giving notes, reworking specific moments repeatedly until you're comfortable, and sometimes completely restaging the piece.

"Don't just stand by your table. After that second coin, pretend you see one near the stage edge and rush to get it. Then there's one in the audience. Let's change tactics from moving to each coin—act like you're sneaking up on one, then perhaps calling another to you."

"OK, the magic effects work, and the performance rhythm. But I don't feel like we have enough conflict, yet. I don't know what your character wants, except to show off that you can pull coins from the air."

113

Getting to the Heart of It

Now we're getting down to brass tacks. The director helps you discover what your magic is really about and how to make it more than a clever trick. This collaboration can get exciting quickly. You discover ways to add character, build and overcome conflict, use pauses, whispers, shouts, and varying rhythms to enhance your story. You learn where the piece starts emotionally, where it climaxes, and all the twists and turns within. This is rewarding creative work.

You **can** do this work alone. But a good director will help you move faster, have more fun, and ultimately create better magic.

Choreographer

If the word "choreographer" makes you think of slinky Bob Fosse dancers, you're not alone. But a choreographer does far more—they set all dance and often all other movement for a show, including yours as the magician. The choreographer understands the power of different movement styles and how to synchronize them with music or dramatic beats. Ballet choreographers, Broadway dance specialists, fight choreographers, stunt choreographers—each brings specific expertise.

Working with a choreographer sometimes means learning to move to counts first—"five, six, seven, eight!"—then transferring that movement to music so it appears to emerge from and sync with the score. Music and movement together can create amazingly powerful emotional responses.

Building Your Physical Vocabulary

As a magician, I would highly recommend that you take at least one or two dance or movement classes. Martial arts, yoga, and ballroom dance all work well. The goal: become more in touch with your body and learn to work intelligently with teachers and choreographers. Your body and voice are your instruments. Make them as responsive and expressive as possible.

Chapter 5: The Team

Stage Manager

In theatrical or corporate venues, you will work with stage managers. Their job is exactly what it sounds like: they manage everything that happens on their stage. They'll tell you where your props can be placed onstage and in the wings, and they'll coordinate with the crew to make sure you get what you need—tables, lighting, sound, and more.

Beyond that, the stage manager runs your technical rehearsals and performances. They call every cue on headset, ensure that the crew hits those cues, and keep rehearsals and performances starting and ending on time. Sometimes a stage manager comes with the venue or event; other times you may provide your own. In many of my clients' shows, I served as stage manager because the performers worked largely without speaking, which meant dozens of cues were triggered by visual moments. If you haven't seen the show before, those visual cues are hard to learn quickly, but I knew them well—often because I had helped create them.

In most theatrical productions, a stage manager writes cues in the margins of the script: when the actor speaks a certain line, cue 21 is taken. In Jeff McBride's show, it might be, "When the red mask appears, we go to cue 15." I knew exactly when that red mask would appear, but teaching a local stage manager all of those visual signals — often a dozen or more within a minute — all for a one- or two-night run, would have taken far too long.

Whatever performing situation you find yourself in, get to know your stage manager. In most cases, they are effectively in charge, and your success will depend heavily on their actions. Make them your allies.

And if you're thinking, "I only work special events; I don't deal with stage managers," think again. There is always someone in charge of the event's flow. At a company party, for example, someone decides when cocktails end and dinner begins, or when everything pauses so the boss can speak. That person will tell you when and where you perform, show you your dressing area, and ask about your technical needs. For all practical purposes, that person is your stage manager.

Set, Costume & Props Designers

Many magicians go their entire careers without ever working with a set, costume, or props designer. That can work, but these collaborators can dramatically elevate the quality and coherence of a show. Even if you never hire dedicated designers, you cannot avoid having sets, costumes, and props—so getting help from someone with real design training can ensure everything onstage supports the purpose and theme of your show.

Audiences respond differently depending on the world you place your magic in. A routine framed in an ornate Victorian ballroom feels completely different from the same routine on a bare stage. Playing your act "in one" in front of the main curtain creates a different energy than standing center stage on a large set backed by a projected night sky.

Although you may not often have the luxury—or budget—to work with a professional set designer, once you reach a certain level, those opportunities will appear. The more varieties of theater you've seen from the audience, the better you'll understand how stage design can support and enrich your work.

So get out and see as much as you can: plays, dance, opera, experimental theater. Visit museums, explore different cities, and actively collect visual experiences. You are a magical theater artist, and the richer your mental library of images, spaces, and styles, the stronger your own work will become.

Lighting Designer

A lighting designer, like a set designer, works with you and the director to shape the overall experience of your show. Scenes may play in full stage light or in narrow pools, and the color and quality of light will shift with the mood you want each piece to create. A good lighting

Chapter 5: The Team

designer illuminates not just you but the world around you, because the environment profoundly affects how audiences respond. As a performer, your focus is on yourself and your audience; as producer and director of the experience, your concern extends to everything they see and feel.

The lighting designer is also your point of contact with the technicians who run the show. They decide where instruments are hung, what colors or gobos they use, and how each cue behaves. Does a lighting change fade in over five or ten seconds, or snap on instantly? Do the stage lights slowly dim while you remain isolated in a single spotlight? These decisions are made by the lighting designer in collaboration with you and your director. It is always a shared, iterative process.

Designing lighting combines the technical and the artistic in a wonderfully covert way. To begin, the designer must sit in on rehearsals, read the script if there is one, and study the set design—ideally with a 3D rendering. They meet with the director to understand the vision and objectives for each moment of each piece. Only then are they ready to think seriously about how to light each beat of the show.

From there, the designer considers every moment in detail. What is this moment about? What are the key images? What emotions should the audience feel? How should they perceive the character or characters onstage—warm and welcoming, tense, mysterious? One scene might begin with the performer in a tight pool of light from a single overhead spot, then gradually widen to reveal a moonlit field and starry sky. Another might call for bright "club" lighting with sweeping and flashing beams. Sometimes moving, flashing light adds energy; other times, the best choice is a subtle, steady atmosphere that lets the scene play without the lighting calling attention to itself.

Once the artistic intentions are clear, the practical work begins. The designer determines how many instruments are needed, where to place them, what colors or pattern gobos they require, and whether each should be sharply focused or soft. This information is captured in a

Wired for Wonder

"hang" sheet: a groundplan of the stage showing every instrument and its position, accompanied by a list describing the type of unit and any extras like gobos or color media. When you arrive at the theater, the crew uses these documents to install and focus the lights.

With the rig in place, the designer builds the actual cues. A cue sheet describes each change: what action or line triggers it, how long it takes, and what exactly happens. Often, the same document includes sound, spotlight, and special-effects cues, because the stage manager will use that sheet to call the show. Everything must align precisely so the technical elements support the performance as one unified experience.

Magic Props Designer or Supplier

Do your props look like they came straight out of the Abbot's magic catalog, or like finely crafted parts of the world you're creating onstage? They can be both, depending on your style, but it is worth considering. The key principle with theatrical and magical props is this: they do not have to be what they appear to be, but they should convincingly look like what you're pretending they are. Clever paint, lighting, and construction can make plastic or foam read as mahogany, and a cheap metal cup read as solid gold. It is the illusion that matters, and a good prop designer understands how to build that illusion in service of your story.

Magic dealers often sell tricks with scripts that match the default look and feel of the props. But you may want to use that same gimmicked prop to tell a very different story. Perhaps the piece you want to perform is a steampunk, industrial-age tale, and the commercial prop you rely on is bright orange and covered with Chinese characters. You still need that particular method, but you want an object that looks like it belongs in your chosen aesthetic. What to do?

There are two main options. First, you can hire a magic prop builder to recreate the entire prop in the style you need; if you have the time, budget, and contacts, this is usually the best solution. Second, you can

Chapter 5: The Team

keep the basic prop but repaint and dress it so it appears to be something else. If you are handy, you may be able to do this yourself; if not, your local theater community probably includes someone skilled at this kind of work who can help without breaking the bank. Either approach leaves you with a prop that truly fits the story you are telling—and may also inspire a bit of envy from your magician friends who are still using theirs "right out of the box."

Theater Manager

In professional theater, two key roles shape where and how a show happens: producers and theater owners. Sometimes one person fills both roles. Theater owners (or venue managers) rent their spaces to producers, much like a hotel manager renting a ballroom or a convention center booking a trade show hall. They are in charge of the venue itself.

In theater, the owner or manager oversees building maintenance, permits, the box office, front-of-house staff, and often the local stage crew. As a producer, you typically rent the space, pay for local personnel (even though they are not your direct employees), and reconcile box office receipts at the end of the run. Most venues also provide a house manager, responsible for opening doors, taking tickets, supervising ushers, and handling the audience's experience before and during the show.

Theater managers are tasked with enforcing local rules and regulations. Some jurisdictions regulate nudity onstage. Nearly everywhere has strict fire codes: open flames, pyrotechnics, and even fog effects are tightly controlled. Fire marshals can inspect a venue at any time and have the authority to shut it down immediately if exits are blocked, equipment is unsafe, or a production is violating fire regulations.

As a touring performer, you may not handle all of these issues directly, but you do need strategies for working with local stage crews, house staff, and venue management. Sometimes you arrive with your

Wired for Wonder

own full crew capable of running your show; other times you depend entirely on local technicians and front-of-house personnel. You need to know which is true for each venue well in advance.

If you want to understand more about how a theater runs, reach out to a local community theater or touring house and volunteer. Theaters almost always need ushers, and that role gives you a first hand view of box office operations, cleaning and turnaround between shows, and, if you ask, the house manager's checklist and routines before the audience is admitted.

Box Office Treasurer

Think of the box office as the part of your team in charge of selling tickets and handling incoming money. The Box Office Treasurer is the person (or system) that can update you on sales from the moment tickets go on sale until the curtain goes up. Once sales close, they generate a report showing how many tickets were sold, at what prices, and what was paid—and in many cases, they are the ones handing you the check for your portion of those sales.

Today, ticketing is often handled online, and there may not be a physical box office at all. This is less common in formal theaters and more typical in hotel ballrooms, conference centers, and similar venues—and of course it doesn't apply at all to restaurant or street work. In those situations, you are effectively your own box office manager.

There are a few key conversations to have with your box office or ticketing contact. First: what they tell people about your show. This is one of your audience's earliest points of contact, and you want that message to be accurate and appealing. Provide a short description they can read on the phone or post online, along with a simple FAQ: Is the show suitable for children? How long is it? Do you use strobes or fire? Without this, they will improvise answers, and those answers are unlikely to be as clear, accurate, or flattering as what you can supply.

Chapter 5: The Team

You can quality-check this easily. Call the box office anonymously and ask about your show. You'll know immediately whether they are using the description and information you provided.

It is important that you have a way of checking the figures that the box office reports. One way is to count the audience members (have one of your team assigned to this task), then compare your headcount to the ticket sales report. If they don't match, you have a problem.

House Manager

The House Manager is the one at the theater in charge of ticket takers, ushers, cleaning staff and the like. They decide when to let your audience into the theater, handle unruly customers or other audience emergencies. Like everyone else here, you want them to be your friends!

Remember, even if you're a solo performer who has created all your material, designed the sound, props, costumes, etc… this is a collaborative art. Everyone involved has the power to make it a better or worse experience for your audience, and, ultimately, we're all in the experience business. Do everything you can to make sure everyone supports you in creating the experience you want your audiences to have!

Producer

Producing is the best and worst job in the theater. A strong producer needs a broad understanding of every aspect of production and every role in the theater. The producer holds most of the power—and all of the ultimate responsibility. As a performer, sometimes you will produce your own shows; other times you will work for or alongside a producer.

Here are just some of the tasks that fall on a producer: choosing the show and venue, hiring everyone involved, arranging rehearsal and performance spaces, coordinating travel, making deals with theaters and other venues, setting up public relations and advertising, overseeing rehearsals, performances, and ticket sales—virtually everything. The producer also has to raise the money to pay for all of this, communicate with investors, and make sure that income is collected and payments go out correctly to artists, crew, vendors, and backers.

Those are only the responsibilities that come immediately to mind. Producing can be deeply rewarding, especially when you partner with your performers: when the show opens and succeeds, you can see and celebrate every good decision and every hour of work that went into it. The trade-off is that you no longer get to do many of the individual jobs you may have loved earlier in your career. After spending years learning how to perform those roles, stepping back to coordinate them instead can be both satisfying and bittersweet.

Chapter 6

Putting it all Together

Here is an example of how everything I've discussed might come together when creating and performing a single piece of magic. I've worked extensively on this piece, though as I write, it's not performance-ready. I'll describe it as if it were complete.

The Effect

The Professor's Nightmare is a classic rope routine where three ropes of different lengths mysteriously transform into equal lengths, then return to their original sizes. Bob Carver won the IBM Originality Trophy for it in 1957. The trick was inspired by Hen Fetsch's "Rope Session with Hen Fetsch" (1954) and "Quad Ropelets" (1955). Similar effects appeared even earlier—Tom Osborne advertised a version in 1935, and Carlyle's "Three To One Rope" appeared in 1936 in *Genii Magazine*.

In its simplest form: the magician shows one short, one medium, and one long rope. He holds them so the top ends show equally above his hand while the hanging ends differ. He lifts the lower ends into his hand one at a time so all six ends show equally, creating three uneven loops below. The magician grabs three ends in each hand and "stretches" them to show all three are now equal length. Sometimes the magician restores the original lengths; sometimes he merges all three into one rope.

The bare-bones story: three objects of different sizes become the same size, then return to their original state. The process is circular—you could repeat the transformation indefinitely. If you want to build a story around this trick, that's your plot skeleton. The beauty is that ropes serve as metaphors for many things: objects, efforts, emotions – even time. This is also a trick that "packs small but plays big"—you can carry it in your pocket but perform it for audiences ranging from one to a thousand.

Wired for Wonder

When creating stories for magic effects, the first step is defining the bare bones. Many effects can be seen from different perspectives. With Professor's Nightmare, I think the core is simple: things that seem different can also be seen as the same, depending on perspective.

The characters represented by the ropes can vary widely. My friend Walt Anthony told a tale of a Chinese merchant with three daughters—one large, one medium, one small. The ropes became ties for their robes. When suitors came calling, the merchant could make his daughters appear different sizes than they actually were. The story had magical transformations and a happy ending.

But remember: the ropes can represent almost anything: lengths of time, amounts of money, companies, pets. Tell us "This rope represents X," and we'll accept it.

My Application of the Effect

I've been considering adding The Professor's Nightmare to a talk I give about reality bending and innovation for business audiences. Perhaps the ropes could represent different workers or parts of a struggling startup.

Before exploring story possibilities, I must master the mechanics. I need to learn and practice every moment. First: displaying the three different ropes, with or without audience inspection. Second: the setup where we gather the uneven ends before "stretching" them to one length. Third: showing all three ropes, apparently one at a time, now equal. I've seen performers do this flawlessly and others badly. It seems incidental but is key to creating conviction. I'll practice it more than feels necessary. Finally: the moment when equal ropes revert to different lengths.

Because my presentation goes through all of the phases several times, I'll practice them individually first, then in sequence, cycling through repeatedly.

Chapter 6: Putting it all Together

Once I feel competent to go through all the moves without thinking, I'll finally be ready for "discovery" rehearsals.

The Script

Assuming I'm fully practiced, here's the story I want audiences to remember. This is a first draft, and will undoubtedly change:

"THREE STRANDS" A Magic Performance

MOVEMENT I: "The Partnership"

(The Wizard enters with three ropes)

WIZARD: Ladies and gentlemen, a story in three—
Three partners, one startup, one destiny. I'll play the part of the Wizard - the CEO!

(Holds up long rope)

Meet Arny Ambitious—he reaches too far,
His hunger's a wildfire, he's chasing the stars.

(Short rope)

And here's Tommy Timidity—brilliant, but small,
He's got all the answers but whispers them all.

(Medium rope)

And this is Libby Laborer—she carries the weight,
She binds the others together, she won't let them break.

Three souls, three lengths, three partners combined—
But watch what occurs when their worlds collide.

MOVEMENT II: "Alignment"

WIZARD: Day One: Arny promises, "We'll own this whole space!"
Tommy knows better but won't show his face.
Libby says, "Partners, together we'll fight!"

(Ropes become equal)

125

Wired for Wonder

And look—they align overnight!
They seem to be equal, one goal they all strive.
But something gets lost as three egos revive!

MOVEMENT III: "The Breaking"

(Sharp movements; ropes return to different lengths)

WIZARD: *Month Three—and it's chaos:*
Arny's exploding—(Long rope wild)
"Three products! Five markets! Keep going!"

Tommy's imploding—(Short rope crumples)
"It's all too much! I warned you we'd fail..."

Libby's fading—(Medium rope strains)
"I can't hold you both—I'm breaking!"

(Voice drops)

Three ropes at war with their own design,
The startup's in freefall—almost out of time.

MOVEMENT IV: "The Truth"

WIZARD: *(Quietly intense)*

Then Libby does the thing that changes it all—
She stops. She refuses to catch one more fall.

"Arny—your drive is tearing us thin.
Tommy—your silence is killing us.
And me? I'm drowning trying to win."

(Pause)

And something breaks open.

Arny: "I'm afraid we'll never scale."
Tommy: "If I'm wrong we'll fail."
Libby: "I thought I could hold it together."

(Ropes become equal again)

And look—
When truth comes,

Chapter 6: Putting it all Together

When masks fall away—
They balance. Not forced. But chosen. Real.

MOVEMENT V: "The Union"

(Building to climax)

WIZARD: But here's the real magic—
Not three separate people, but this—

(THREE ROPES BECOME ONE—held high)

THIS!
One startup. One vision. One rope in my hand.
Not because they were all the same—
But because their differences made the company's strength!

(Final flourish)

Arny's reach, Tommy's mind, Libby's heart—
This is where magic and business both start.

Production

That's my initial outline script. I'll start discovery rehearsals, improvising through it several times, then recording. Days later, when satisfied, I'll send it to two or three mentor friends for director's notes. Because it's designed for business groups, I'll adjust for different audience sizes and whether I'll have PowerPoint behind me.

For full professional production values, I'll find royalty-free music and record two tracks: one for PowerPoint presentation, one audio-only. I'll rehearse repeatedly with the music until I can perform it almost like choreography, without cueing starts and stops.

I'll also create two or three lighting cues. The piece begins in full stage light. The wider stage may fade slowly to darkness while a single pool rises—strong backlight and narrow front light. This peaks just before I hold up the unified rope. Then blackout after the bow, with full stage light restored two seconds later.

Wired for Wonder

Once I've rehearsed the piece 20 or 30 times with full production, I may hire the services of a director as I begin getting it in front of an audience. I expect we'll find ways to build in more conflct, and to use a bit more audience interaction, both of which will improve the piece.

The director may give small polishing notes, or see major flaws and we'll rework the whole thing together, winding up with a polished piece that I hope will inspire the crowds of business leaders it is designed for.

I hope this gives a different, perhaps more practical perspective on the various aspects of magic theater I've been discussing, in theory, throughout the book.

Chapter 7
Theater Adjacent: Shows Online

Zoom Shows

Not long ago, the COVID-19 pandemic restricted us all to our homes, making live shows impossible in most places. But many performers—including my friends Paul Draper and Jeff McBride—wanted to continue working—so we figured out ways to do shows over the internet.

I'll speak specifically about Zoom shows here, though these comments apply equally to platforms like Livestream, Google Meet, and similar services. The key criterion: they must allow interaction. Otherwise, you're just performing live television, and the specific advantages of theatrical conditions don't apply.

Because the Zoom interface—camera, microphone, and internet connection—differs fundamentally from a theater where audience and performer share physical space, it pays to have a technician, engineer, or stage manager handle that interface for you. You have enough to do performing and tracking all those tiny faces on your screen.

Your stage manager admits audience members to the meeting, controls when they can speak, runs audio and video clips that support your show, spotlights you and volunteers, and more. As always, a great stage manager can make all the difference in the quality of the overall experience for both you and your audience.

A Hybrid Medium

This format isn't precisely theater because audience and performer aren't in the same physical space. Neither is it film or traditional television, which aren't interactive and typically require large crews and budgets impractical for the solo performer working for a small audience. Zoom shows are hybrids, unique in that way. I've watched numerous magic shows on Zoom, each with different strengths and weaknesses.

You can produce your show with television or video production values—changing camera angles, combining long and close shots—if you have the resources. You'll probably want to do this for some pieces. Just as in live performance, not every piece uses an audience volunteer, and you can insert pre-recorded segments with higher production values into an otherwise live, simply produced show. Variety improves the experience. These segments also give you a moment to breathe, re-set, or whatever else you may need to do, without having to pause the experience for your audience.

Unlike traditional TV, you can see and interact with your Zoom audience. You won't want their microphones on constantly—extraneous sound creates distraction. But your engineer can control access, and you can tell them when you want mics on. When you need an individual volunteer, they can be "spotlighted" onscreen next to your image, and you can talk with them almost as if sharing the same space.

The Applause Problem

The medium has one significant issue: audience response. If everyone leaves microphones on, the result is cacophony. If mics stay off, you hear nothing. We developed a partially workable solution: we taught audiences to applaud by raising their hands and wiggling fingers at the screen. This made applause visual, visible to performer and other audience members alike. It was also easier than Zoom's built-in solution, which requires clicking an applause icon, then turning it off.

Production Considerations

Because you'll appear on a screen, you want to learn basic cinematography and how to compose that screen image. Lighting

Chapter 7: Theater Adjacent - Shows Online

remains just as important as in any theatrical show. Ensure sufficient light for a clear camera image. How you're lit—color, position, everything—sends subliminal messages about who you are, the show's formality, and what emotions you want audiences to feel. If you can arrange multiple camera angles or settings, that will help maintain interest.

Watch and learn from television and film. How often do scenes change? What's the effect of underscoring? How long do scenes typically last? When you watch the best work from a student's perspective, trying to understand how they do it, you can learn an astonishing amount quickly.

Entering Story Space

When does your show start? Has it begun the minute you open your Zoom space? Will you allow your audience to talk as they enter? Will cameras and microphones be automatically on or off? Since this medium is still relatively young from a cultural perspective, will you post written guidelines for audience behavior? Something like the following might work:

> *"Welcome to my show! As you enter, please make sure your camera is on and that we can all see your face. Microphones are currently turned off to avoid excess noise, but feel free to chat in the chat window and say hello to friends.*
>
> *Microphones: During the show, your mic will be turned off by our host most of the time. However, when you're asked to participate, we'll ask you to turn your mic on. You'll see the microphone icon in the lower left corner of your screen. Once our stage manager starts the show, you can click to turn it on or off.*
>
> *Cameras: This is an interactive show, so it's important for us and your fellow audience members to see your face! We want to see you laugh and enjoy the show with everyone else. Please leave cameras on unless you need to step away briefly.*
>
> *Applause: Because your microphone will be off most of the time, we won't hear your applause. Instead, hold your hand up to the screen and wiggle your fingers—we'll take that as applause!*

Wired for Wonder

> *Music: There is music playing as you enter. Please adjust your sound levels based on the music. If you can't hear it, you'll have trouble hearing the performance. If it's too loud, the show will seem too loud. Now's the time to adjust.*
>
> *Thanks for joining us. The show will begin momentarily!"*

Or perhaps you're a Renaissance Festival performer relegated to Zoom shows during snowy months. Here's an Elizabethan version (created by Perplexity, my go-to AI assistant. If I were actually using this, I might commission a small animated video of a town crier delivering it):

> *"Good gentles all, welcome to this humble spectacle! As thou enterest, pray keep thy camera's eye open, that we may behold thy fair countenance. Thy voices are presently stilled to prevent cacophony, yet thou mayst greet thy fellows merrily in the written chat.*
>
> *Of Microphones: Our master of ceremonies shall keep thy voice silenced for most of our revels, yet when thou art called to participate, spy the speaking trumpet symbol in the corner of thy screen and be swift to unseal thy voice.*
>
> *Of Cameras: This be a most interactive entertainment! We yearn to witness thy laughter and delight. Leave thy camera lit, withdrawing only if nature urgently calls.*
>
> *Of Applause: Since thy voices sleep, lift thy hand to the crystal screen and waggle thy fingers—we shall take this as thunderous applause!*
>
> *Of Music: Sweet strains now fill our space. Adjust thy magical device that thou mayst hear neither too faint nor o'er loud.*
>
> *We thank thee, gentle souls. The show shall begin anon!"*

Starting the Show

Once it's time to begin, you need a clear transition. An introduction, an entrance, an establishing shot of your performance space—any and all of these signal that the show has started. You're transitioning from that "in between time" when audiences enter the theater to the

Chapter 7: Theater Adjacent - Shows Online

moment the lights lower and the show begins in earnest. If your signaling isn't clear, your audience won't know when the show has started either.

For Jeff McBride's Zoom shows, we ran opening credits as you'd see at the beginning of a movie, followed by a short segment where Jeff's wife Abigail explained how we wanted audiences to behave. Then we introduced Jeff and opened one of several cameras he would perform for.

I've seen other Zoom shows where it wasn't clear when the show started. The performer greeted audience members as they appeared and had small-talk discussions. Once everyone arrived, they decided to begin: "I guess we're all here now. Who wants to see a magic trick?" That's informal and fine, but far less clear. There was no significant transition into the world of the story.

The Medium is the Magic

I'm a huge fan of old movies. The works of Charlie Chaplin, Buster Keaton, and the Méliès brothers have inspired and delighted me since I first encountered them. If you're a magician who hasn't seen the Méliès brothers' work, you're missing some of the most creative magic and film that exists. Part of that magic came from the fact that they didn't know what was possible yet. The medium was new, so they explored everything. What happens if I speed up the camera crank? What if I slow it down? How about putting it on a crane? Let's lock it to a box and roll the box over as the actor dances inside? They tried everything they could think of.

I once saw an interview with Orson Welles about making Citizen Kane. How did he come up with all those creative shots no one else had thought to use? His answer: "I didn't know what I was doing. No one told me 'that's not how we do that.' So we just tried anything we thought would give the effect the story needed." Some of the greatest film of all time was created that way, because the creators still had what Buddhists call "beginner mind."

Wired for Wonder

We're at that stage with shows done on Zoom and other interactive video platforms. Unlike film, costs don't need to be high. We no longer pay for film stock, developing, cutting. You can do it all on your mobile phone today if you're creative. A laptop offers almost inexhaustible alternatives. And with AI increasingly available at little or no cost, you can generate impossible backgrounds and even characters you can interact with. I mentioned earlier that theater is the art form where you make more choices than any other, because it uses all the other art forms. This is even more true for this new hybrid form that combines interactivity and live performance with all the possibilities previously only available in film or commercial television.

Experiment with the Medium

If you're doing your show on Zoom, please experiment! Take advantage of all the possibilities. You can run short video clips while setting up for the next piece. You can change backgrounds—one piece in your workshop, the next on a beach or city street. Think of your favorite movie. It probably jumps around in space and maybe time to tell its story. Why not do that in your Zoom show? Changing scenes does much of the work of maintaining audience interest and adds color to the experience.

I remember, when the pandemic was still strong, a relatively well-known magician collaborated with a theater company to produce his show online. The show was all card tricks in one location—before his close-up table in what appeared to be his kitchen. It was, I think, ninety minutes, but for me it felt endless. I don't remember any specific tricks, and if I hadn't been "in the business" wanting to learn about this new medium, I would have left. Sure, he had stories with his tricks, but there was no variation in theme, no change of scenery, no real rhythmic change. Don't be that performer—unless you're performing for other magicians so interested in every nuance that that's enough. For the general public, it's not.

Taking Advantage of the Screen

One of my favorite magic pieces ever was Penn & Teller's "upside

Chapter 7: Theater Adjacent - Shows Online

down" performance on SNL. The screen opens with them sitting side by side at what looks like a news desk. Things look normal, but when one lets go of a pen, it flies away. The other is busy holding his cup down on the desk. Mayhem ensues—hysterical and baffling. Then the camera pulls back and rotates, revealing they're upside down, strapped to their seats. Suddenly all those magic moments are completely understandable—but still vastly entertaining.

This is "taking advantage of the medium." Your audience has certain assumptions, and the camera/screen interface makes it easy to exploit those assumptions in ways impossible in real life.

Here are two magic techniques made possible by the camera/screen interface, and not really available in live performances.

First: The camera is just one eye. This may not seem like a big deal, but it means stereo vision and depth perception are gone. Optical illusions like Jerry Andrus' "Parabox" require you to close one eye for them to work—but they work brilliantly on camera.

Second: Green screen tricks—just like those used to create special effects in major films for decades—work live on Zoom. A piece of cloth the same color as your green keying background becomes an "invisible" screen that can cause objects to vanish and appear simply by placing it over them or removing it. It's like black art, but green for the camera.

These and other bits taking advantage of camera/screen limitations make effects possible in a Zoom show that would never work live.

Learn from TV and Film

If you're going to be on screen, learn from those who have done it before. Watch popular television shows. How often do they "cut" from one shot to another? Why do you think they do that?

I'll tell you. It's for two reasons: different points of view help direct interest and tell your story. The second is less flattering to us humans:

we have short attention spans. We want "something new" every few seconds. Action movies average about 25 camera cuts per minute, while interview programs like Charlie Rose average only about 5 cuts per minute. Even baking shows have increased their cutting pace over the years—early seasons of The Great British Bake Off averaged about 20 cuts per minute, while recent seasons hit 28-34 cuts per minute.

Having a second camera that covers just your hands and props, and being able to cut between that and a longer shot including your face and upper body, is one way to make this work. You can also use tools like OBS to bring in different scenes, still images, and recorded video, all without spending a fortune.

When producing Jeff McBride's show for Zoom, this was one of our concerns. When he performed close-up pieces, we sometimes wanted attention on just his hands; other times it was important to see his face and how he reacted to the magic himself. Sure, we could have him move his camera to change the shot, but that felt amateurish when we tried it. So we got a second camera and figured out a way for our engineer, Scott Steelfyre, to switch between cameras from his studio across town. I should note that we had the luxury of having produced a once-a-week interview show for magicians on Zoom for quite some time, so we were perhaps better equipped and more experienced with Zoom production than most. But the truth is, you can achieve most of the effects we did with just one or two cameras and a laptop.

Get an Engineer or Video Director

I know I'm repeating here, but this is important: Having the engineer or video director on board is the one thing I'd advise not doing without. Their job doesn't need to be difficult or complicated, but as a performer you really don't want to split your attention between camera switching, letting people into and out of the Zoom room, turning mics on and off, and performing. This person will do all that for you. You want to concentrate on your performance and on interacting with all those faces on the screen.

Chapter 7: Theater Adjacent - Shows Online

The good news? You can train an interested, somewhat tech-savvy friend to do all of this in just an hour or so. Pay them $100-200 per show, and you have a partner. All theater is about the magic of collaboration, and Zoom shows are no different. Get an enthusiastic support team, and you'll be a happy performer.

Don't Forget Interactivity

I've been going on about techniques and video-specific things you can do, but please don't forget that interactivity with your audience is what makes magic so special. Be sure to work as much of that into your Zoom show as you can. When possible, use one or two volunteers. Solicit audience response and acknowledge it. If you can enlist the aid of a "stooge," you can rehearse and manage to seem to pass an object from your screen to theirs. You might consider sending an envelope with a prediction to someone before the show, so they can open it on screen at their location. Anything you can do to build the sense of really interacting with the audience will enhance their experience of the show.

Like any other show, your Zoom show needs a clear beginning, middle, and end. If you can build a theme throughout, create some conflict, and resolve that conflict, you'll find that your audiences appreciate—and remember—and talk about—the experience you give them.

A great way to learn how to do this without telling traditional stories is to watch great comedians doing their live sets. They're easy to find on streaming services, and you'll learn about theming, callbacks, and other useful techniques you can apply to your magic. As when performing onstage, you want your audience to know when the show begins, have some idea how it will progress, and know when it's over and what it was all about. Just a string of tricks performed on your kitchen table won't do it. Running characters and themes will.

Wired for Wonder

Zoom Tech
Equipment

For Zoom, you can get along with very little. A good, professional-level camera is essential. For meetings, the mic and camera on your laptop might suffice, but if you're charging people to see you perform, spend money on a professional-level webcam and microphone.

I just checked Amazon (it's July 2025) and found the webcam I use, the Logitech C920x HD Pro, for about $70, and my microphone, the Samson Go Mic clip-on USB, for just $40—hardly budget-breaking prices. I'm using these now partly because I'm in a nomadic phase, and both are small, but produce professional results. When living in Vegas and on Zoom for hours daily, I used a higher-resolution camera and studio-level microphone, but I'm not sure people at the other end would have noticed the difference.

My friend Doug Conn likes to use an Insta360 cam for his podcasts because he can set up multiple "views" and switch between them using the software that comes with the camera. The Insta360 has a 360-degree surround field of view at very high resolution, but you can select parts of it as different views. This saves you from needing multiple cameras to show, for example, a full-body shot and then just your hands.

Backgrounds

I like to use keyed backdrops. I can appear to be in my library for one scene and on a beach for the next, all without leaving my desk chair. Zoom's keying/virtual background feature is excellent, but if you're using another service like OBS, you'll have more difficulty getting a clean key effect. Great, relatively bright lighting helps, as does a real green backdrop. But Zoom's backgrounds just work, even without perfect lighting or a green screen. On the other hand, if you live in a house with multiple fascinating magical areas, as Jeff McBride does, you might want to move around and share different scenes, as we did when we produced our Zoom shows during the pandemic. You'll need cameras and setups in each location, so this can be more expensive, but we felt it was worth it.

Lighting

Learn about television studio lighting. Yes, lots of "influencers" use just a single 'ring light' to make themselves look like fashion models. I'm amazed at how many don't know that the reason a ring light is shaped as it is, is so the camera can shoot through the center. If you're not going for that particular effect, another light will do just as well.

I prefer the kind of "key" and "fill" lighting used in most TV studios: more focused and slightly "warmer" lights from one side, and softer, "cool" lights from the other. Set up at roughly 45 degrees from either side, and not too high an angle. I buy clip lights at the hardware store and use warm and cool LED bulbs in them—not too bright—with little cloth diffusers I got cheaply on Amazon. You can adjust brightness by moving your lighting closer or farther away, so you don't really even need dimmers.

As I travel, I simply find a place in the hotel room or apartment where this situation already exists—perhaps near a window on one side and a desk lamp on the other. You can tell when it's right by looking at your image on the screen.

If you can arrange some kind of backlighting for your Zoom setup, you'll usually be happier with how you look on screen. Again, don't spend a lot on this. A smaller clip light from somewhere above and behind you works well. Even locating yourself beneath an existing overhead light that's a bit behind you can enhance your look. Don't use that as your only light, though, unless you're going for a strange dramatic effect. Experiment until you get the look you like.

Here's another thing about lighting for video: we don't change it as often as we might during a stage performance. For Jeff McBride's 70-minute casino shows, we often had as many as 180 lighting cues. For the same length show on Zoom, we probably had 3 or 4 different "looks." Get the look right for your camera and scene, and leave it.

Wired for Wonder

Audio

Zoom and other streaming video services are mostly set up to filter out ambient room noise. This is great for meetings, but not so much if you're relying on background music or sound effects. Because the services have matured, they've made concessions for different situations and allow you to turn on "original sound" or turn off "ambient filtering." If you can't hear your background music properly, ask Google or search for tutorials about your particular platform. There are hundreds of videos that will help you get your settings right.

Record Rehearsals

One of my favorite things about Zoom is that I can set myself up for a show, get everything in place, then record myself as a test and play back what I've recorded. Do I like the sound? If not, make an adjustment. Is the lighting right? The balance between my face and my background? All of those things become obvious when watching what you've recorded. So record, play back, and make adjustments until you're happy with the results. Then you're ready for your audience.

Creating Rhythm

When performing in a theater, we often alternate "in one" scenes in front of the main curtain with larger, more spectacular scenes that take up the full stage. This creates a natural rhythm: big, small, big, small. The constant change helps keep audiences engaged. I recommend something similar for your Zoom show. Alternate between single image—just you filling the whole screen—with gallery view and scenes where it's just you and one or two others on the screen. Also, plan a couple of short video clips, as they'll give you a moment to catch your breath during the show. You can choose to tell your audience they're about to watch a video — or not. It's a magic show—they don't have to know everything.

Conclusion

If there is one idea I hope you take away from *Wired for Wonder*, it is this: Magic is, unequivocally, a deeply theatrical art. My own journey, which began with a nervous performance of tricks from *The First Book of Magic* taught me the electric power of audience connection, a feeling of adulation and transformation that is truly the magic of theater.

This book has been about that essential intersection, drawing on my 35 years spent working in theater and later alongside the world's finest magicians like Jeff McBride and Marco Tempest, to show the theatrical craft required to transform a clever trick into a profound magical experience. The "right" magicians understand their purpose isn't just mild amusement; it is to create moving stories that force the audience to question the limitations of their perceived reality.

You may still insist you are not a storyteller, but honestly, whenever you confront a live audience, they take away a narrative. Your job, therefore, is simply to ensure the story they take away is a good story! To achieve this, you must apply critical performance skills: acting, voice, movement, and improvisation.

We have established that a magician is "a very special kind of storytelling performer, playing a character with magical powers". This role demands that you consistently 'break the fourth wall', acknowledging your audience as characters and active participants in the narrative. The story your audience takes away isn't about fictional people; it's a story that happened to them!

The entire process, from story creation (complete with conflict) to the final bow, is fundamentally about making choices. The blessing is that every choice grants you control that can make the experience more magical. The curse is that your audience experiences those choices

Wired for Wonder

even if you haven't consciously made them. Remember: EVERYTHING COMMUNICATES.

Whether you perform in the chaos of the street, the intimacy of a close-up table, the rigors of a casino showroom, or the cutting-edge interactivity of a Zoom production, your goal remains the same: to provide your audience with an experience that makes them believe.

By embracing the discipline of the actor, utilizing every element of stagecraft (set, props, costumes, sound, and lighting), and learning to collaborate with a strong support team (like directors and stage managers), you ensure that your magic is about more than "the adventures of the props in the magician's hands".

Go out, keep learning, and keep experimenting. The master performer is consistent, and their worst night will be better than the talented upstart. The world is waiting to be wired for wonder by your art.

Conclusion

Wired for Wonder

END PAGES

Acknowledgment and Thanks

A special thanks to Phil Ackerly and Douglas Conn, who generously shared their time and wonderful knowledge in interviews here.

Less directly, but no less important: My clients for nearly 35 years, Jeff McBride and Marco Tempest. These two are true masters of theatrical magic, always exploring, always improving. It has been a joy working with them to better understand how we do what we do. They demonstrate every day what it means to be continually learning, continually growing and continually improving.

I also want to thank my personal support team, which includes Sylvia Brallier, Kat Rettke, Donna Courtney and Kevin Lepine. Always there to help me stay on course, hear crazy new ideas, and provide valuable feedback. You make my life better every day. And, of course, my mother, Margy Beckwith and brother Timothy Beckwith, who have both contributed so much to my own ability to think independently.

Finally, thanks to our magic community. I've reached out many times for your input on particular ideas, cover designs, and more, and you've always provided valuable feedback and information. I hope this book repays some of your efforts!

More from Tobias Beckwith

Books for Magicians

Beyond Deception, Vol. 1

Beyond Deception, Vol. 2

Beyond Applause

Books for Personal & Business Transformation

The Wizards' Way

The Wizards' Way to Powerful Presentations

The Performer's Edge

The fastest way to find these books is to go to Amazon and search "Tobias Beckwith."

Web Sites

Tobias' Personal Site - tobiasbeckwith.com

Wizards for Business - wizardventure.com

Magic & Magicians - yourmagic.com

Business for Performers - beyondbeyond.me

Link Page for Tobias Beckwith:

www.tobiasbeckwith.com/links-for-tobias-beckwith/

Index

Ackerly, Phil 15–20
Acting 3, 67, 70–83, 87–89, 97, 98, 141
Agon 58, 59
Amplification 16, 36, 50, 109
Aristotle 58–61
Articulation 88, 91, 92
Audi TT 52–54
Audience 1–5, 7–35, 37, 39–51, 53–61, 63, 65, 66, 68–73, 75–81, 83, 87–89, 94–98, 100–105, 107, 109–114, 117–122, 124, 127, 130–134, 136, 137, 140–142
Backgrounds 134, 138, 140
Blackstone 7, 8, 18
Burger, Eugene 12–14, 40, 56, 79, 83, 95
Busking / Street Performing 23–25, 27, 28, 30–33, 35–37, 39–43
Cellini, Jim 25, 28, 32, 43
Character 2–5, 10, 11, 22, 58, 59, 61–64, 66, 69, 71–77, 79, 81, 83, 88, 89, 124–128, 134, 137, 138, 141
Choreographer 4, 73, 82, 109, 111, 114, 128, 142
Color 4, 32, 33, 35, 36, 65, 107, 117, 118, 120, 131, 132, 134
Conflict 4, 30, 54, 58–61, 76, 77, 114, 116, 126, 137, 141, 142
Conn, Douglas 24, 25, 33–36, 41, 138
Costumes 3, 7, 10, 22–24, 32, 35, 36, 52, 55, 56, 81, 83, 84, 103, 111, 113, 115, 116, 119, 121, 122, 142
Creativity 49, 64–66, 134, 135, 137
Director 111–114, 117–119, 127, 131, 136, 142
Draper, Paul 49, 129
Eye contact 17, 18, 69–71, 98, 101

Wired for Wonder

Family Shows   3, 14–18, 20, 21, 41, 42, 56, 58, 80, 110, 111
Fourth Wall (Breaking of) 2–5, 7, 17, 18, 27, 100, 101, 107, 112, 141
Houdini, Harry   62, 63
Improvisation   3, 7, 17, 18, 95, 96, 130, 134, 141
Instrument (Body as)   76, 80–82, 85, 87, 117
Jobs, Steve   65
Keynote Speaker 45, 49, 50, 55, 69
King, Mac   20, 93, 94
Lewis, Bobby (Lewis Method)   71, 72, 83
Lighting   3, 4, 10, 15, 22, 23, 47, 57, 58, 68, 69, 80, 82, 102–113, 116–121, 128, 131, 132, 139, 140, 142
Magic Castle   44, 45
McBride, Jeff   2, 10, 16, 21, 22, 24–26, 30, 37–39, 43, 45, 46, 49, 52, 57, 58, 61, 64, 81, 84, 98, 101, 104, 109, 110, 116, 129, 133, 134, 136, 138, 140, 141
Meisner, Sanford 89
Movement   3, 21, 23, 32, 33, 35, 36, 42, 59, 71, 73, 76, 80, 81, 84–87, 91, 92, 94, 96, 100, 109, 111, 114, 115, 117, 118, 125–128, 141
Music   3, 4, 16, 19, 21, 26, 32, 35, 36, 46, 48, 50, 51, 64, 66, 102, 110, 111, 114, 117, 118, 128, 131, 132, 140
Oedipus   62
Plot   53, 59–63, 124
Producer   45–52, 109, 117, 119, 121, 122
Professor's Nightmare   64, 123, 124
Props   3, 4, 10, 12, 13, 16, 20, 23, 31, 32, 35, 37, 46, 54, 56, 57, 61, 63, 64, 79, 81, 83, 84, 88, 93, 94, 96, 103, 108, 111–113, 115, 116, 118–120, 122, 123, 126, 127, 131, 135, 136, 142
Rehearsal 2, 21, 23, 34, 47, 48, 81, 93–99, 101, 104, 109, 111, 112, 115, 117, 118, 120, 122, 125, 127, 128, 131, 137, 140, 142
Robert-Houdin, Jean Eugène   4, 74, 76, 77
Script   3, 4, 23, 26, 34, 53, 80, 82, 89, 93, 94, 109, 112, 117, 118, 121, 125, 127

END PAGES

Siegfried and Roy   9, 20, 56, 103
Sound   3, 4, 10, 16, 21, 23, 31, 32, 35–37, 41, 46, 48, 50, 51, 53, 57, 76, 77, 80, 81, 85, 89, 90, 91, 101, 102, 103, 108–112, 115–118, 120, 121, 122, 128, 130–132, 140, 142
Stage Manager   68, 110, 115, 116, 118, 130–133, 136, 142
Stanislavsky, Konstantin   71
Storytelling   2–4, 7–13, 15, 18, 21, 22, 24, 25, 28, 29, 31, 34, 35, 37, 41, 46, 47, 49, 50, 52–61, 63–66, 71, 73, 74, 76, 77, 79, 83, 88, 89, 94, 97, 100, 114, 116, 118, 119, 121, 124, 125, 127, 131, 133, 137, 141, 142
Tempest, Marco   10, 38, 45–48, 52, 53, 107, 141
Theme   58, 60–63, 107, 113, 116–118, 122, 124, 125, 134, 137, 139
Trade Show   28, 40, 45, 49–52, 56, 119, 122
Transformation   1, 2, 4, 22, 56, 60–62, 100, 102–104, 106, 123, 124, 141, 142
Venue   3, 4, 8, 10, 12, 15, 16, 21, 23, 34, 45, 47, 48, 50, 51, 55, 56, 99, 101–105, 111, 112, 115–117, 119–122
Voice   3, 4, 10, 12, 15, 16, 19, 31, 36, 37, 41, 49–51, 59, 70, 73, 76, 77, 80–82, 85–94, 96, 109, 117, 126, 141
Warm-up   81–83, 85–87, 89–93
Zoom   129–140, 142

Wired for Wonder

www.ingramcontent.com/pod-product-compliance
Lightning Source LLC
Chambersburg PA
CBHW071832230426
43672CB00013B/2823